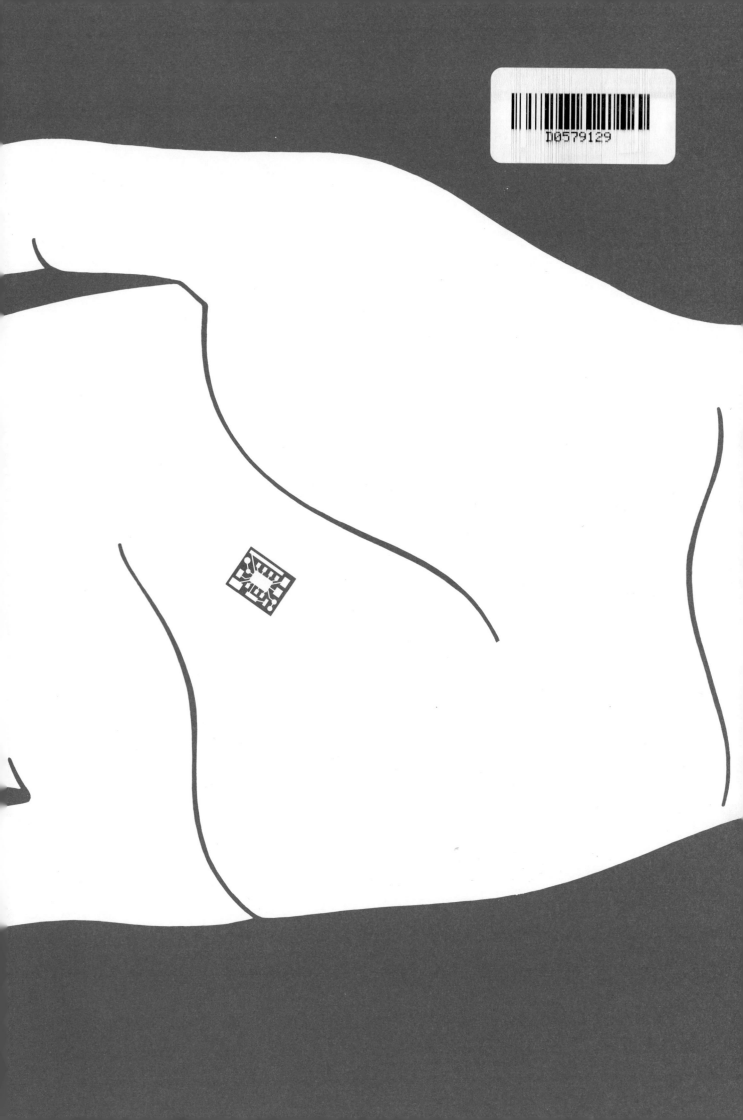

Computer Age

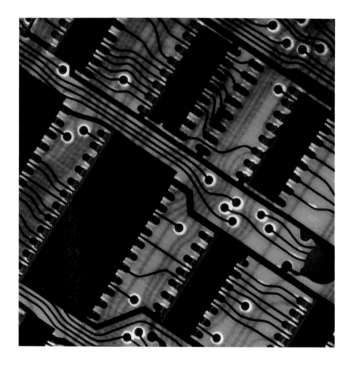

TIME-LIFE
ALEXANDRIA, VIRGINIA

C O N T E N T S

5 Digitizing Daily Life 84

6 Computer Networks 108

7 Science and Computers 130

1
History of the Computer

Since earliest times human beings have used numbers. Even the most primitive tribes made complex calculations that were needed for agriculture, trade, and navigation. Devices to help with such calculations began with the prehistoric use of stone counters and progressed with the abacus.

Not until the seventeenth century did German and French tinkerers invent a better instrument, the first adding machine that functioned with interlocking cogs and wheels. In the nineteenth century, Englishman Charles Babbage designed a steam-powered machine that could calculate square roots, cube roots, and other exponential functions. Although Babbage never developed this "Analytical Engine" beyond the model stage, he applied many of the same principles used in modern computers.

With the advent of electricity came electric calculators based on punch cards and relays. The first modern computer was not the work of any one person but the result of experiments of the 1930s and 1940s in England, the United States, and Germany. The Electronic Numerical Integrator and Computer, or ENIAC, built with vacuum tubes at the University of Pennsylvania in 1946, is the best-known early computer.

In the last 50 years, computers have entered daily life in more ways than people ever could have imagined. This book will examine how these machines work, with a look in this chapter at the ingenious inventions that led the way to computers.

The earliest calculating tools built a solid base for the modern computer, from counting stones, the abacus, Napier's rods, the Pascaline, and punch cards to the vacuum tubes in ENIAC, one of the first electronic computers.

mille   Cartainne   dixainne   Nanbre
                                                     Cinple

How Did Early Civilizations Do Math?

The history of math began when people had to keep track of quantities that were larger than one. Early nomadic tribes counted and recorded the animals in their flocks though they had no written number system. To count, they picked up pebbles or grains and put them into a bag. For large numbers they used different fingers to symbolize the numbers 10 and 20. They developed the concept of a number as a symbol separate from the thing being counted.

As recordkeeping and reckoning became more complex, people invented tools to help in the process. The abacus was one of the earliest tools. Although its origin cannot be pinpointed, the abacus is known to date back to early Greek and Roman times. At first the abacus was a sandy surface, a wax tablet, or a slab of rock with marks to indicate number positions and pebbles used as counters. Romans called such pebbles *calculi*, from which the word *calculation* is derived.

By the early Middle Ages, the Oriental abacus, a boxlike frame holding beads on rods, appeared in the Middle East. It is still widely used in the Soviet Union, the Middle East, and Asia.

■ **Roman counting tablet**

Pebbles rest in columns above and below a dividing line marked with Roman numerals. Each pebble below the line in the column farthest to the right counts as one unit, and each pebble above it represents five units. When the total reaches 10, one is carried to the left. The table shows the count for 256,317 sheep.

Earliest calculator

The ancient abacus from the Greek island of Salamis is a 5-foot-long marble slab, believed to have been used in a temple by moneychangers. The inscription lists number values and names of coins, such as drachmas, talents, and obols.

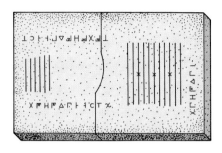

The first computer

The Chinese abacus consists of a wooden frame divided into an upper and lower section. The rods correspond to columns and the beads to numbers.

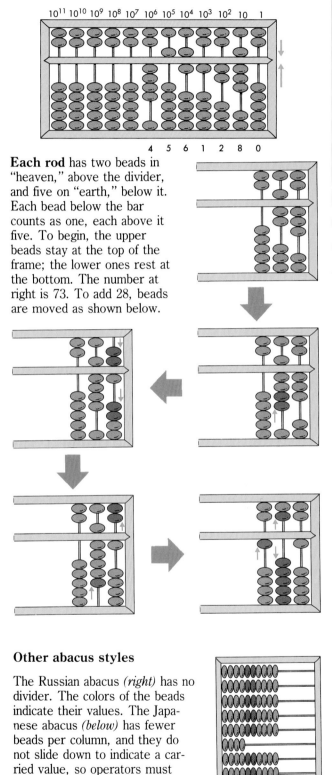

Each rod has two beads in "heaven," above the divider, and five on "earth," below it. Each bead below the bar counts as one, each above it five. To begin, the upper beads stay at the top of the frame; the lower ones rest at the bottom. The number at right is 73. To add 28, beads are moved as shown below.

Other abacus styles

The Russian abacus *(right)* has no divider. The colors of the beads indicate their values. The Japanese abacus *(below)* has fewer beads per column, and they do not slide down to indicate a carried value, so operators must keep a mental tally of anything carried to the next column.

Russian abacus

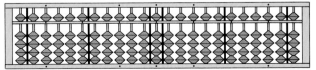

Japanese abacus

Who Invented the First Calculator?

The intellectual ferment of the seventeenth century drove mathematicians to great heights with inventions to ease the lot of those who labored endlessly over calculations. In 1614, John Napier, a Scottish theologian and mathematician, discovered logarithms and transformed complex multiplication problems into simpler problems of addition. Inscribing multiplication tables onto a set of rods in 1617, he further simplified multiplication of large numbers. Within a few years, Napier's logarithms came to be used on the slide rule, and that made his rods obsolete.

In France in 1642, Blaise Pascal, the 19-year-old son of a tax collector, experimented with a mechanical adding machine to help his father in his work. He devised a machine driven by interlocking gears that could calculate large numbers. Although Pascal's invention, called the Pascaline, became widely known as the first adding machine, a German professor, Wilhelm Schickard, actually built the first calculator in 1623. Another German, diplomat and mathematician Baron Gottfried Wilhelm von Leibniz, replaced Pascal's invention with a more easily operated calculator in 1673.

Pascal's remarkable invention

The Pascaline

The machine, shown below in cross section, adds or subtracts when cogwheels interlink as they are turned. A wheel carries a total greater than nine to the next column. The result appears in the display window, with the numbers at far right for addition and right for subtraction.

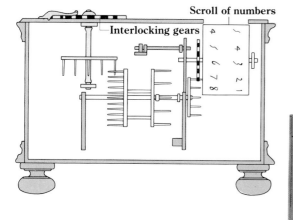

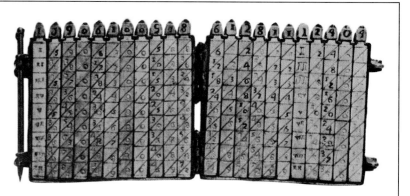

Interior view of a six-digit Pascaline

Napier's rods

John Napier constructed multiplication tables on thin rods, or blocks. Each side of a block carried numerals forming a mathematical progression. Manipulating the blocks made it possible to find square and cube roots and to multiply or divide large numbers. Mathematicians do not regard the rods as Napier's greatest contribution to science. Although the rods were used all over Europe, he became better known for his invention of logarithms.

With a twist of a dial Pascal's invention made math easier. The upper display windows showed additions and the lower ones subtractions.

Movable slat for addition or subtraction

Dials set numbers to be added or subtracted.

mille

dixaine de mille

Cantainne . dixainne

nanbr' cimple

Blaise Pascal (1623-1662) penned this advertisement: "I submit to the public a machine . . . by means of which you may, without any effort, perform all the operations of arithmetic, and may be relieved of the work which has often times fatigued your spirit."

Leibniz's calculator included a hand crank that drove stepped wheels to speed up multiplication and division.

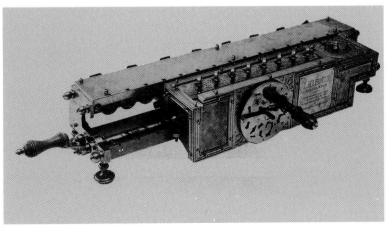

9

Who Conceived the First Computer?

In the nineteenth century, long before the arrival of the age of electronics, Englishman Charles Babbage came so close to developing the functions of a computer that today he is known as the father of the computer.

The first machine built to Babbage's specifications, the Difference Engine, was powered by a steam engine. It calculated logarithm tables by the method of constant difference and recorded the results on a metal plate. The working model he produced in 1822 was a six-digit calculator capable of preparing and printing numerical tables. In 1833, Babbage announced plans for a more powerful and versatile machine, the Analytical Engine. He designed the new machine to perform a wide range of computing tasks from a store of 100 40-digit units. A mill, which was composed of cogs and wheels, would manipulate the numbers, just as an operator would instruct the machine or, in more modern terms, program it by punching a series of cards.

The idea of punch cards was not new. French silk weaver Joseph-Marie Jacquard had first thought of them for his automated silk loom. So well had Jacquard refined the technology that the weaving of an intricate silk pattern required instructions punched on 10,000 cards. Unfortunately, the technology of Babbage's time did not match the remarkable machinery he designed. He was never able to complete the Analytical Engine, yet Babbage had conceived the fundamental principles of the modern computer.

Visionary Charles Babbage (1792-1871) devoted his genius to calculating machines. He also helped found the Royal Astronomical Society and held the same Cambridge chair of mathematics that Isaac Newton once occupied.

The Analytical Engine

Store

The Difference Engine

A working model of the Difference Engine, constructed from Babbage's notes 100 years after his attempts, gleams with shiny gears and dials.

Babbage's design of the Analytical Engine contains some of the features found in modern computers. Punch cards carried the operating directions and data; the machine's mill did the work of a central processing unit. The result, or output, went directly onto metal printing plates. The machine shown below is a partial reconstruction from Babbage's drawings.

Jacquard's loom

Even inexperienced operators of this silk loom could weave complicated patterns simply by changing the punch cards.

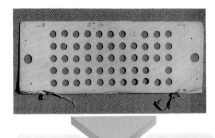

Three sets of punch cards fed information into the machine. Operation cards and variable cards contained operating instructions; number cards held data.

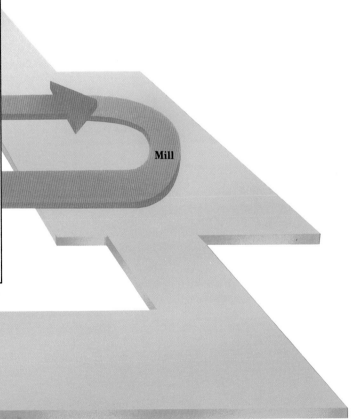

The silk loom followed a preset pattern, as in a program.

Punch cards are arrayed as in a program.

A model of the Analytical Engine

Mill

Output

Output device

Babbage's design included an output device, but it was never built.

How Did Herman Hollerith Advance Computer Technology?

Herman Hollerith built what has been called the world's first data processor to count and tabulate the U.S. 1890 census. The story of his accomplishment began at a time when waves of settlers from the East opened up the West. As a special agent for the U.S. Census of 1880, Hollerith studied the painfully slow procedures of the count. An army of clerks labored manually for years to tally the 1880 data. By the time workers analyzed, organized, and published the figures, they were more than five years out of date. Building on the idea of punch cards, Hollerith devised cards, the size of dollar bills, with 12 rows of 20 holes that indicated a person's age, sex, country of birth, marital status, number of children, and the like. Canvassers collected census data and transferred the answers to the cards by punching the appropriate holes. They fed the cards into a tabulating machine, and each time a pin found a hole, the information registered on a bank of recording dials. In time, the machines counted and tallied information on 62,622,250 persons for the U.S. Census of 1890.

Hollerith later improved his invention by adding functions to the equipment. The company he founded to manufacture the machines became part of the corporation known today as IBM.

Card counter

Card reader

Card punch

Census card punch

The ingenious method of encoding cards with information used the simple device below. The operator pushed a lever with a pin at one end in the slot with the desired information *(bottom);* this caused a second pin to punch the card *(top)* in the corresponding spot.

Punch card

Herman Hollerith (1860-1929) received the contract for the 1890 census when he demonstrated the speed of his machine. The population had grown by more than 20 percent since 1880, but his machines cut the time of the count from five years to two.

The automatic card feeder sped up the count.

Hollerith's statistical machine consisted of four parts: a card punch that perforated cards at predetermined points, based on census forms; a card reader to check the position of the punched holes; a card counter that displayed the number of each hole as the wheels of the counters turned; and a card sorter to separate the cards according to the holes punched.

○ Punch card system

The system at left processed stacks of cards. The cards were put in a box with a weight on top, then each one was pushed into place so that it could be counted.

Card sorter

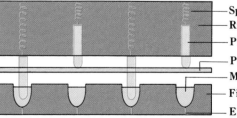

The card reader

A rising metal plate, covered with small pins attached to springs, pressed against a fixed metal plate. A punch card between the plates was read when a pin went through a hole and touched a pool of mercury, completing an electrical circuit.

- Spring
- Rising plate
- Pin
- Punch card
- Mercury
- Fixed plate
- Electrical contact

What Was the First Electronic Computer Like?

The ideas of Charles Babbage became reality 70 years after his death when Harvard University researchers led by Howard Aiken began work on the Mark I calculator in 1941. The Mark I used banks of electromechanical relays that served as on and off switches. Overall, the Mark I measured 8 feet by 50 feet. The machine could complete in one day math problems that took a person six months to do with an adding machine, performing three operations per second. But the Mark I was soon outpaced by the Electronic Numerical Integrator and Computer (ENIAC), dependent on vacuum tubes for switches. J. P. Eckert and John Mauchly of the University of Pennsylvania unveiled the new computer on February 14, 1946. The ENIAC could compute a thousand times faster than any previous machine, performing 5,000 addition and subtraction, 350 multiplication, or 50 division problems per second. But the ENIAC also was about twice as large as the Mark I. The enormous machine filled 40 cabinets with 100,000 components, including some 17,000 vacuum tubes; weighed 30 tons; and measured 18 feet by 80 feet.

Harvard's Mark I

Relays controlled the Mark I. Each relay had a contact anchored at a pivot point. The spring at one end kept the contact open. When current flowed through a coil wrapped around an iron bar, its magnetized core attracted, or pulled, the contact, closing the circuit. Current then flowed along the arrow-marked path.

Closed circuit · Contact · Coil

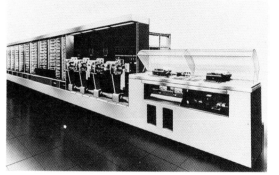

The Mark I went into service in 1944.

Comparing size to performance

ENIAC vastly outperformed its predecessor, the Mark I, but was dwarfed by the computing power of the Cray-1, a supercomputer introduced in 1975. The boxes below show the relative sizes and speeds.

1 Cray-1

2 ENIAC

3 Mark I

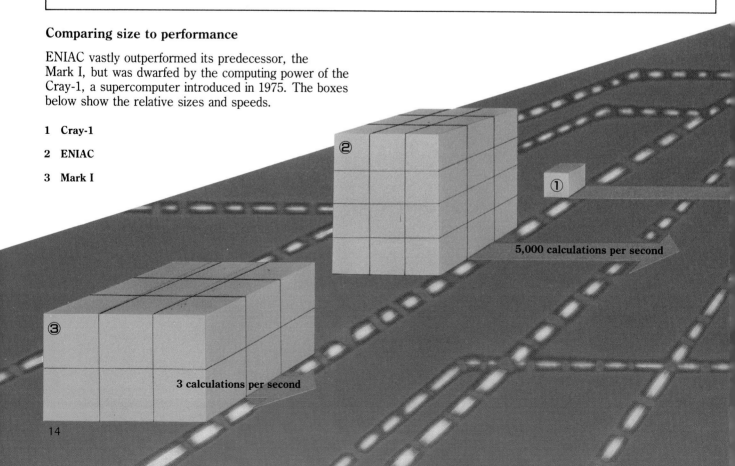

5,000 calculations per second

3 calculations per second

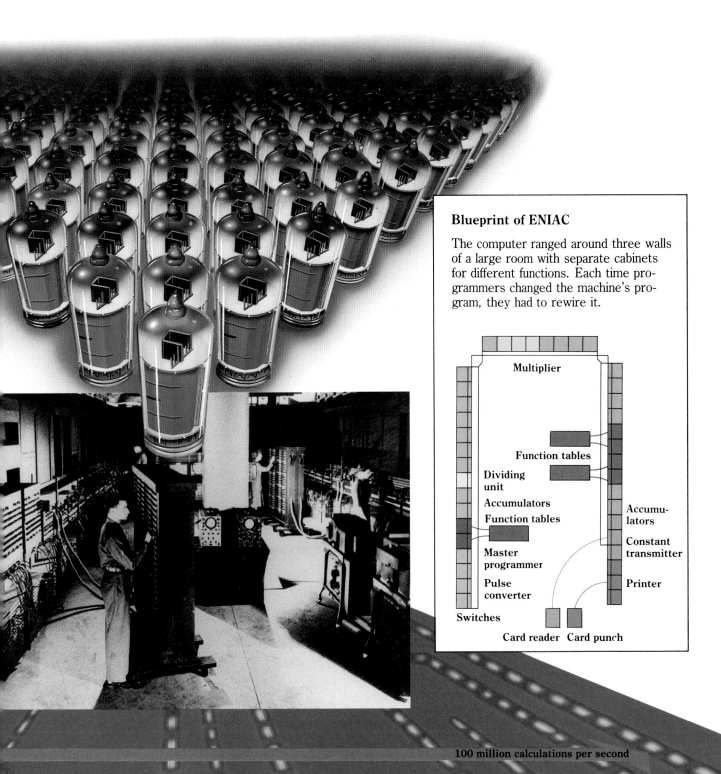

Blueprint of ENIAC

The computer ranged around three walls of a large room with separate cabinets for different functions. Each time programmers changed the machine's program, they had to rewire it.

Multiplier

Function tables

Dividing unit

Function tables

Accumulators

Function tables

Accumulators

Master programmer

Constant transmitter

Pulse converter

Printer

Switches

Card reader   Card punch

100 million calculations per second

Cray-1

The Cray-1 was the first of the supercomputers, faster and more powerful than previous generations. The earlier computers ran on vacuum tubes, transistors, or integrated circuits, but the supercomputers depend on very-large-scale integration devices.

2
Modern Computers

In the years since 1946, when the Electronic Numerical Integrator and Computer, or ENIAC, was built, computers have changed greatly. Advances in design have made computers faster and smaller, and they can do more than calculate numbers. In most parts of the world, computers coordinate traffic lights, run factory assembly lines, and coordinate the takeoffs and landings at airports. They handle bank deposits, bills, and other financial transactions, or instantly calculate midcourse corrections for a rocket taking a satellite into orbit. Some supercomputers—enormously more powerful than ENIAC—fill a whole room, but there are microprocessors small enough to pass through the eye of a needle. Pocket calculators and many wrist watches contain these tiny computers.

What all these machines have in common is the ability to perform simple tasks with numbers—such as adding or comparing—at lightning speed. This chapter will examine modern computers—their internal structure, their working methods, and the devices that help people use them—to see how they accomplish these tasks.

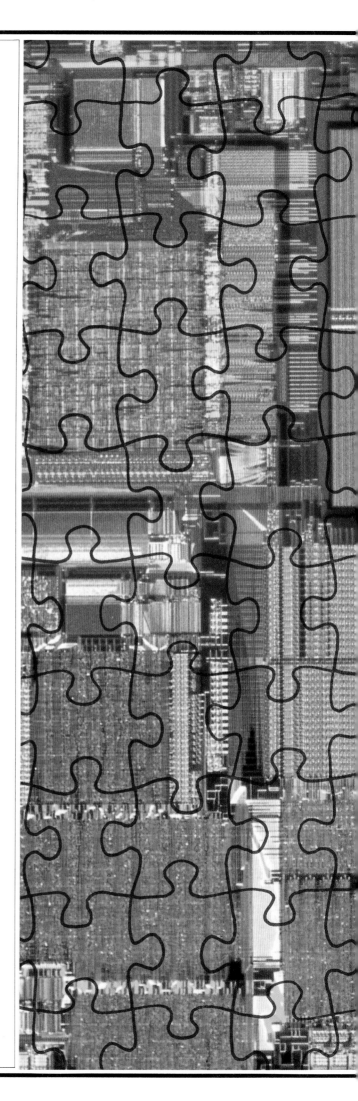

Like a jigsaw puzzle, the complex microprocessor chip in the illustration at right must have all its parts present and in their correct places. A mistake in even one of the chip's many circuits would keep it from working properly.

What Are the Parts of a Computer?

The physical parts of a computer are known as its hardware. The computer system shown below is a mainframe, a powerful system used by big businesses and government agencies. It fills a room, and its parts are linked by cables laid under the floor. But computers that fit on a desk top *(opposite, top)* can also accomplish all the tasks done by the computer shown below.

The basic layout and linking of a computer's parts is called its architecture. The brain is the computer's central processing unit, or CPU. This intricate electronic circuitry performs the computer's tasks when it handles data. The CPU's arithmetic logic unit (ALU) and control unit carry out the computations and coordinate the movement of data and the execution of instructions. Taken together, the instructions that tell a computer what tasks to perform are known as its software. Linked to the CPU is a memory unit that contains the computer's operating instructions, or program.

An input device, such as a card reader or keyboard, lets the computer receive data. Similarly, the computer needs an output device so people can see the results of its work. The mainframe's printer puts the results on paper, but the most common output device is a monitor, which resembles a television screen. Input and output are so closely related that experts lump them together as input/output, or I/O.

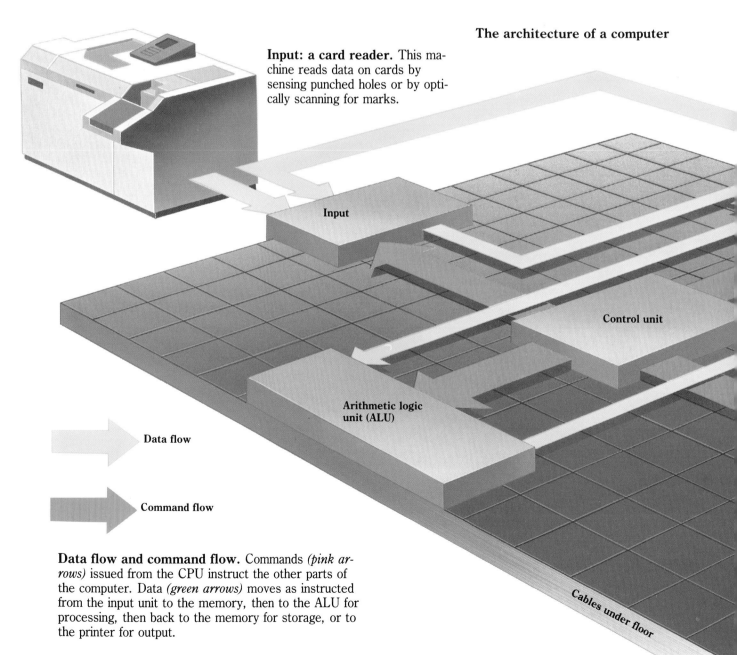

The architecture of a computer

Input: a card reader. This machine reads data on cards by sensing punched holes or by optically scanning for marks.

Input

Control unit

Arithmetic logic unit (ALU)

Data flow

Command flow

Cables under floor

Data flow and command flow. Commands *(pink arrows)* issued from the CPU instruct the other parts of the computer. Data *(green arrows)* moves as instructed from the input unit to the memory, then to the ALU for processing, then back to the memory for storage, or to the printer for output.

A personal computer

A personal computer, or PC, packs all its functions into one cabinet and takes up little space; PCs also are affordable. In a typical setup, a main unit contains the CPU and memory, as well as I/O in the form of one or more floppy-disk or hard-disk drives. A keyboard, monitor, and printer are attached; many systems include a mouse. PC performance has improved greatly between the 1970s and 1990s.

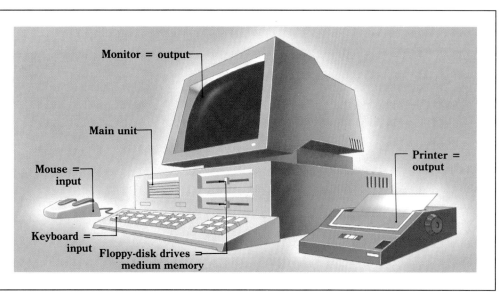

Monitor = output

Main unit

Printer = output

Mouse = input

Keyboard = input

Floppy-disk drives = medium memory

Data storage on a magnetic-disk drive. Data is stored by a head moving over a spinning magnetic disk. The head writes and reads data almost instantly.

Data storage on a magnetic-tape drive. Data is written by one head—which magnetizes a metallic coating on the tape—and read by another.

Peripherals

The many devices that can be connected to the computer are called peripherals, because they attach to the edge, or periphery, of the CPU. I/O peripherals include XY plotters to print graphs, devices that recognize and produce speech, and optical scanners to "see" text. Memory devices include compact disks that store 600 million numbers and letters.

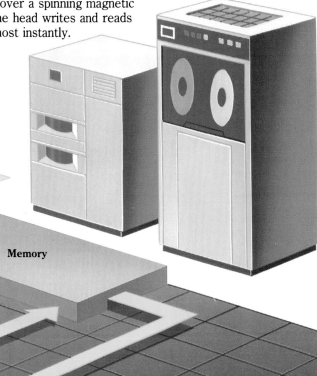

Memory

Output

Output: a line printer. By printing a whole line at once, this machine prints data on paper fast, perhaps 1,000 lines a minute.

What Is an Integrated Circuit?

In the earliest electronic computers *(pages 14-15),* the circuit components that performed operations were vacuum tubes. These bulky items, resembling electric light bulbs, used a lot of electricity and gave off a great deal of heat. The transistor, invented in 1947, changed all that. This little device used semiconductor material, so called because the same material either transmits or resists electricity, depending on whether the semiconductor itself has an electric current flowing through it. With this new technology, all kinds of electronic switches could be built on small, flat wafers, or chips, of silicon. Transistors enabled computer designers to build circuits in smaller spaces and run them on much less electricity. For more powerful computers, circuit designers combined ever-larger numbers of transistors onto single chips of semiconductor material in what are called integrated circuits, or ICs.

Transistors today are microscopically small, and the circuitry of an IC chip is contained on a piece of semiconductor material only a fraction of an inch square. The little blocks that can be seen mounted in rows *(below)* on a printed circuit board, or PCB, of a computer are ICs enclosed in plastic cases. Each chip contains a multitude of simple circuit elements, or devices. Most of these are transistors. ICs can also include diodes, which let current flow only one way, and resistors, which block it.

IC chips mounted on a PCB

Personal computer, or PC

20

No moving parts. Inside the computer cabinet, rows of ICs in their protective cases, as shown below, are mounted on a printed circuit board *(green)*. Each of the pale green lines is a printed electrical pathway; together they form "buses" carrying current among chips.

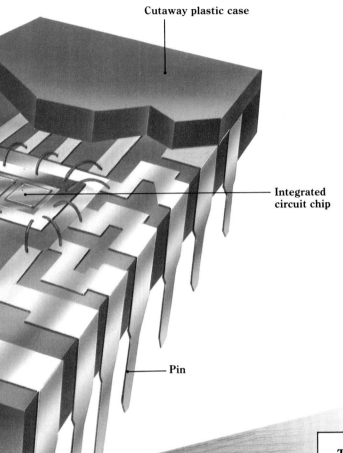

Cutaway plastic case

Integrated circuit chip

Pin

Bus

Tiny connectors. At the edges of a chip, shown here greatly magnified, wires as fine as human hairs carry electrical signals to and from the chip's circuitry. These gold or aluminum wires resist corrosion and carry electricity well.

Transistor anatomy

Transistors—the basic, microscopic units of electronic circuits—are switches that are turned on or off by electric current. Tiny metal pathways *(gray)* carry current *(red and green arrows)* to and from these devices. Arranged in combinations called logic gates, transistors react to electrical impulses in different, predictable ways, enabling the computer to handle a broad variety of tasks.

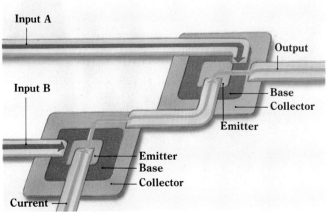

Input A

Input B

Output

Base
Collector

Emitter

Emitter
Base

Collector

Current

A logic gate. Only if input current *(red arrows)* arrives to activate the base *(red square)* in each transistor can the supply current *(green arrow)* flow to the output wire.

What Do Integrated Circuits Do?

Computers are built with two types of integrated circuits: logic and memory chips. Logic chips are used in the arithmetic logic unit (ALU), where calculations are made, while memory chips hold data and programs. There are many types of logic chips, some simple, others very complex; the microprocessor chip *(below, far right)* that serves as the central nervous system of a personal computer is a good example of a complex logic chip. Often both logic and memory functions are combined in a single chip.

The microprocessor serves as the computer's central processing unit (CPU), combining the controller and the operating logic. Other chips near the microprocessor include the clock generator, which produces the signal that keeps the computer's actions in step; the I/O controller, which coordinates data input and output; and various coprocessors, which are specialized processors that handle only one kind of task, but at

great speed. Additional controller chips handle communication circuits, magnetic-disk drives, and graphics terminals.

Memory chips are either read-only memory (ROM) or random-access memory (RAM). ROM chips retain their stored data even if the machine is turned off; they are used to hold completed programs or data that will not need to be changed. Most RAM chips are volatile, which means that their contents are erased when the computer is turned off or if power is interrupted. The computer can both read from them and write to them—that is, store new data on them.

A motherboard

An integrated circuit device

Enlarged 2,500 times, this n-MOS, for negative-channel metal-oxide semiconductor, is a common integrated circuit transistor. Normally this switch is closed; current *(blue arrow)* cannot cross from source to drain. But voltage *(red arrow)* applied to the gate attracts electrons *(specks)* below, forming a channel that lets current pass.

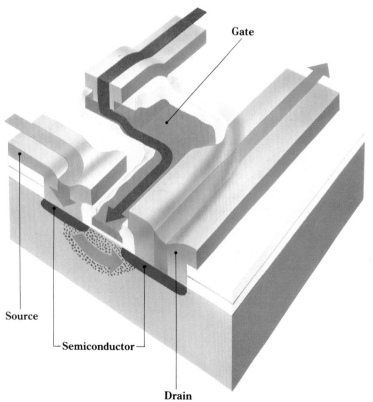

ICs in their packages

Before an IC can be mounted on a PCB, it must be enclosed in a protective case, or package, and provided with external connector pins, or leads. At right are some common IC cases, named for their shapes and their pin arrangement.

A DIP, or dual in-line package, has two rows of pins. An FLP is a flat package with pins on two sides, while a QFP is a flat package with pins on four sides. An LCC, a leadless chip carrier, has no pins, or leads, at all. An SIP, or single in-line package, has one straight row of pins, while a ZIP, or zigzag in-line package, has one zigzag line of pins.

DIP

FLP

QFP

LCC

SIP

ZIP

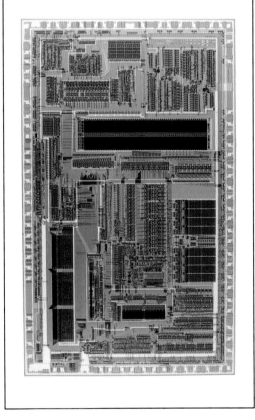

Direct memory access controller

Coprocessor for mathematics

Peripheral interface controller

Central processing unit microprocessor

RAM chips

Slots for additional ROM chips

Cache high-speed memory: RAM chips

7 8 9 10 11 12

13 14 15 16

17

18

A monolithic microprocessor

The chip below contains a microprocessor as well as ROM, RAM, and I/O controllers. Such computer chips are generally used to control machinery and are in many home appliances.

An array of chips. The PCB at left, the motherboard of a personal computer, contains several kinds of IC chips, including a microprocessor, controller chips, and memory chips.

How Does a Computer Do Its Work?

Modern computers are based on the architecture developed in 1945 and outlined on pages 18-19. In this method—the stored program concept—instructions and data are stored together in the memory of the computer. The collection of instructions, known as a program, and the data are loaded into the memory. All memory is divided into individual addresses, so the instructions and data can be found whenever they are needed.

The central processing unit, or CPU, contains the program counter, which makes sure that the program's instructions are carried out in order, one task at a time. After each operation, the program counter advances by one step.

Other CPU components, shown below and right, include the control unit, which directs the step-by-step operations of processing; the registers, which provide temporary storage for small amounts of data; and the arithmetic logic unit, or ALU, which performs additions, subtractions, and comparison operations.

The steps at right explain how the computer moves commands and data to carry out a simple "ADD" command. The program instructs the computer to add two numbers and store their sum—as ordered in the third line on the screen below, which reads "30 C=A+B." Many steps are involved, but each takes only 30 billionths of a second, or less, and calculations are completed very quickly. Although all numbers are in binary form *(pages 26-27)* inside the computer, they appear here in decimal form for easy reading.

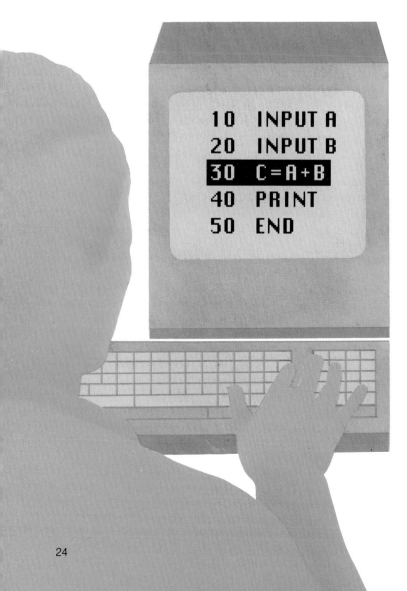

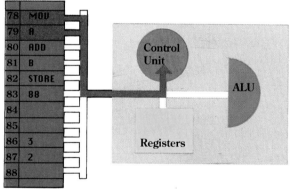

Instructing the computer

The operator has written a short program in the computer language BASIC. The first two lines (numbered 10 and 20 at left) tell the computer to get numbers from the keyboard. The diagrams at right show how the computer executes the third statement on the screen. This statement, "C=A+B," tells the computer to add the quantities A and B, and line 40 instructs the computer to store the result. Line 50 ends the program. In this case, A is in address 86, B in address 87, and C will be put in address 88.

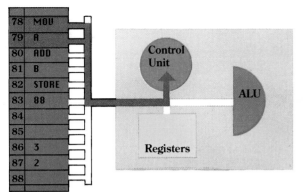

1. First instructions. The control unit retrieves machine instructions from addresses 78 and 79. After decoding the instructions, the control unit knows it must fetch the data from address 86.

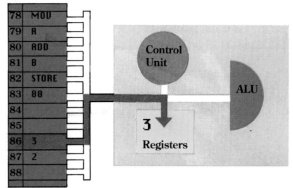

2. Moving the first number. The control unit copies A, the number 3 at address 86, and places it into one of the registers—the temporary storage location for small amounts of data.

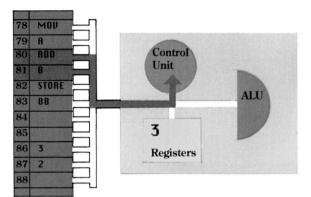

3. Reading the ADD command. The control unit retrieves the next instruction—the ADD command—from addresses 80 and 81 and, in turn, decodes those instructions.

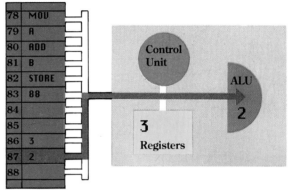

4. Reading the data. Following the instructions, the control unit copies the value of B, which is 2, from address 87 and places it into the arithmetic logic unit, or ALU.

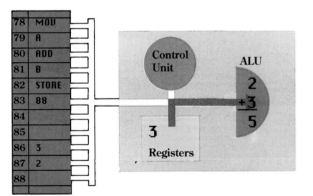

5. Adding the data. The first number is taken from storage in the CPU register and brought to the ALU, where math operations are performed. Then the computer can add the two numbers.

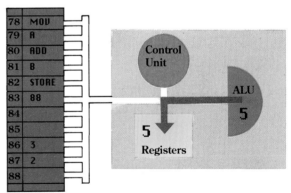

6. Temporary storage. The sum of the addition is temporarily stored in the CPU register until the control unit can check to see what the programmer wants done with it.

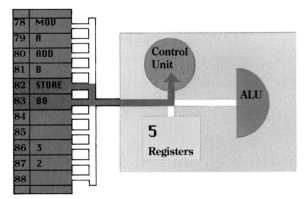

7. Summing up. The control unit retrieves from address 82 the instruction to store the data into memory position 88, where the data will be readily available for any subsequent calculations.

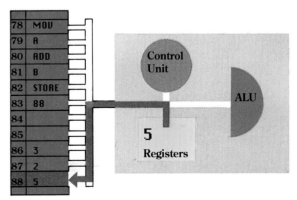

8. Storing. The control unit places the sum, the number 5, into address 88 as instructed, completing eight machine-level operations needed to carry out just one line of a program.

What Is Binary Code?

Everyone knows that computers can perform complex calculations with vast amounts of data and at great speed. But not everyone knows that these feats depend on just two either-or electrical conditions: whether a current is on or off and whether a voltage is high or low. How, then, does a computer manage to process so many different kinds of information?

The secret is binary code. All data fed into a computer is represented by 1s and 0s, which are then assigned one of those two electrical states—1s are on or high voltage; 0s are off or low. Changing data so that it is represented by 1s and 0s is called binary conversion, and the resulting notation is called binary code.

In decimal notation, which is the base-10 system in everyday use, numerical values are represented by 10 numerals, from 0 to 9, and each place in a number has a value 10 times as great as the place to the right of it. To represent the next number greater than 9, decimal notation sets a zero in the ones place and a 1 in the next higher place—the 10s place—to form 10. Similarly, the binary system—a base-2 system—uses just two numerals, 0 and 1, and each place is worth two times the place to its right. Thus in binary code, only 0 and 1 can be shown as a one-place number; any number greater than 1 requires use of two places. After 0 and 1, the next three binary numbers are 10 (read one-zero), 11 (one-one), and 100 (one-zero-zero). Binary 100 is equivalent to 4 in decimal notation. The table at right *(top)* shows other decimal-binary equivalents.

Any number can be expressed in binary code; it just takes a greater number of places than decimal notation. Even alphabets can be written in binary code, using an assigned binary number to represent each letter.

■ Two digits, to four places

Sixteen combinations can be made by using only dark or lighted balls and combining them in sets of four *(right)*. If the dark balls represent 0s and the lighted balls 1s, these 16 sets of balls are a 16-unit binary code, with numeric values from 0 to 15 *(see table, top right)*. Even with only two kinds of balls, binary notation can represent infinite combinations, simply by increasing the number of balls in each group—that is, the number of places in the numbers.

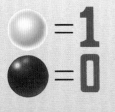

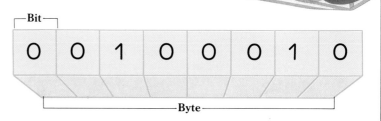

Bits and bytes

The smallest unit in computer processing, a bit is a unit of data that can have either of two possible conditions. Each of the 1s and 0s at right, for example, indicates a bit. A bit can also be represented in other ways: by a current being on or off, by a hole being present or absent, by the direction of magnetization being to the left or to the right. A group of eight bits is a byte. Since there are 256 possible bytes, they can represent up to 256 characters and symbols. Many computers handle data a byte at a time.

┌Bit┐							
0	0	1	0	0	0	1	0

└──────── Byte ────────┘

Binary conversion. A four-digit binary code can represent decimal values up to 15.

Binary	0000	0001	0010	0011	0100	0101	0110	0111	1000	1001	1010	1011	1100	1101	1110	1111
Decimal	0	1	2	3	4	5	6	7	8	9	10	11	12	13	14	15

Part of the ASCII code table

Char								Char							
SP	0	1	0	0	0	0	0	@	1	0	0	0	0	0	0
!	0	1	0	0	0	0	1	A	1	0	0	0	0	0	1
"	0	1	0	0	0	1	0	B	1	0	0	0	0	1	0
#	0	1	0	0	0	1	1	C	1	0	0	0	0	1	1
$	0	1	0	0	1	0	0	D	1	0	0	0	1	0	0
%	0	1	0	0	1	0	1	E	1	0	0	0	1	0	1
&	0	1	0	0	1	1	0	F	1	0	0	0	1	1	0
'	0	1	0	0	1	1	1	G	1	0	0	0	1	1	1
(	0	1	0	1	0	0	0	H	1	0	0	1	0	0	0
)	0	1	0	1	0	0	1	I	1	0	0	1	0	0	1
*	0	1	0	1	0	1	0	J	1	0	0	1	0	1	0
+	0	1	0	1	0	1	1	K	1	0	0	1	0	1	1
,	0	1	0	1	1	0	0	L	1	0	0	1	1	0	0
−	0	1	0	1	1	0	1	M	1	0	0	1	1	0	1
.	0	1	0	1	1	1	0	N	1	0	0	1	1	1	0
/	0	1	0	1	1	1	1	O	1	0	0	1	1	1	1
0	0	1	1	0	0	0	0	P	1	0	1	0	0	0	0
1	0	1	1	0	0	0	1	Q	1	0	1	0	0	0	1
2	0	1	1	0	0	1	0	R	1	0	1	0	0	1	0
3	0	1	1	0	0	1	1	S	1	0	1	0	0	1	1
4	0	1	1	0	1	0	0	T	1	0	1	0	1	0	0
5	0	1	1	0	1	0	1	U	1	0	1	0	1	0	1
6	0	1	1	0	1	1	0	V	1	0	1	0	1	1	0
7	0	1	1	0	1	1	1	W	1	0	1	0	1	1	1
8	0	1	1	1	0	0	0	X	1	0	1	1	0	0	0
9	0	1	1	1	0	0	1	Y	1	0	1	1	0	0	1
:	0	1	1	1	0	1	0	Z	1	0	1	1	0	1	0
;	0	1	1	1	0	1	1	[	1	0	1	1	0	1	1
<	0	1	1	1	1	0	0	\	1	0	1	1	1	0	0
=	0	1	1	1	1	0	1	]	1	0	1	1	1	0	1
>	0	1	1	1	1	1	0	^	1	0	1	1	1	1	0
?	0	1	1	1	1	1	1	_	1	0	1	1	1	1	1

Code tables

When binary code is used to stand for letters of the alphabet or punctuation marks, code tables must be constructed to show which binary number stands for which character or symbol. Several such codes have been drawn up and are in use today. Most personal computers adopt the seven-digit code called ASCII (pronounced "as-key"); the name is the acronym, or initials, of American Standard Code for Information Interchange. The table at right shows some of the ASCII binary codes for the English alphabet.

Other codes have been established to represent the thousands of characters used to write languages such as Japanese, Chinese, or Arabic.

How Is a Computer Able to Add?

All computer calculations are carried out with binary numbers using basic electronic elements, actually different kinds of switches. Some of these switches—AND, OR, and XOR—are called logic elements because each gives a logical, predictable result when using the 0s and 1s of binary code. Because they work by either permitting or preventing the passage of electric voltage pulses—no voltage stands for 0, voltage for 1—logic elements are also called gates.

These gates are similar in that each has more than one input but only one output. The AND gate gives 1 as an output only if all its inputs are 1. Conversely, the OR gate gives 0 as an output only if all its inputs are 0. The XOR gate, on the other hand, gives a 1 as output when its input is a 0 and a 1, and produces a 0 when the input is two 0s or two 1s. From just three elements like these, computer scientists build computer circuits such as the adder circuits diagramed at right, which perform addition.

The half-adder *(top right)* is so named because it can only add two digits in binary code and produce a single digit result or a single digit plus a carry. Because they cannot handle an incoming carry, half-adders are often used as the first link in a group of logic gates. Each full adder *(bottom right)* can handle two digits and a carry and accept a carry from the previous sum in the chain.

Adders handle all math problems, since addition is the basis of all arithmetic operations: Multiplication is repeated addition; subtraction is addition of a negative number; and division is repeated subtraction.

Logic gate input/output

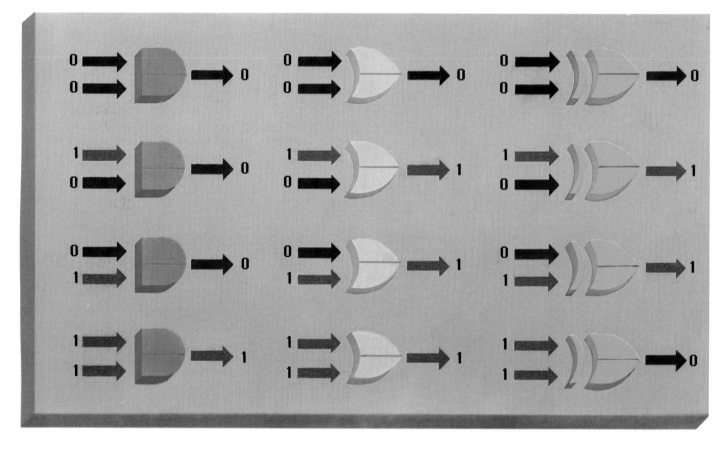

An AND gate will produce a 1 if both inputs are a 1. Any other combination of inputs will render a 0 as output.

An OR gate will produce a 0 if both inputs are 0. If one or both inputs are 1, its output will be a 1.

An XOR gate will deliver a 0 if both inputs are 0 or both are 1. If the input is a 1 and a 0, the output is a 1.

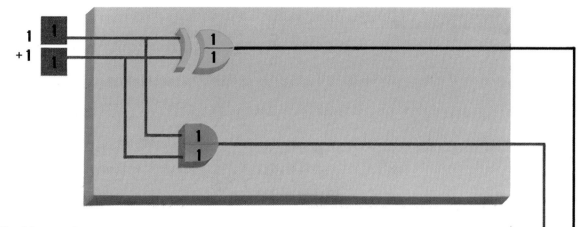

How a half-adder works

The circuit above for adding two single-digit binary numbers consists of an XOR (top) and an AND gate (bottom). Adding 1 plus 1, the top adder channels voltage from both 1s through the XOR gate and puts out a 0. The AND gate also receives current from both 1s and issues a 1. The resulting 10 (read as one zero) in binary code is the decimal number 2.

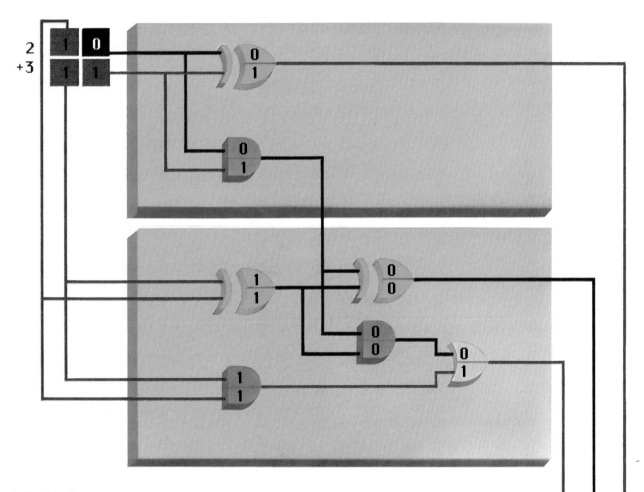

The full adder's use

In combination, the half-adder (top) and full adder (bottom) can calculate larger numbers that involve a carry. To add 2 plus 3, or 10 plus 11 in binary notation, the half-adder begins with the XOR gate and produces a 1. The AND gate generates a 0, which is carried over to the full adder. In turn, the full adder passes the voltage of 11 through its five gates, picks up the carry from the half-adder, and puts out a 1 and a 0. When this is combined with the 1 from the half-adder, the result is 101, or the decimal number 5. For larger numbers, more full adders are used, one for each digit in the binary numbers.

How Does a Computer Store Data?

Laid out in rows and columns, the memory of a computer can seem like an enormous town, but with the same number of houses on every street and all the houses the same size. In most computers, the size of the "house" is eight bits—that is, one byte, enough to store one character. As in a town, each house in computer memory has its own address; but unlike a town's street system, every house in memory is on two streets. As in the picture below, every address is at the intersection of two wires; these are linked to the networks of wires—the buses—on which information travels inside the computer. This part of the network is called the address bus.

Memory addresses, like all other digital infor-

mation, are binary numbers, or "bit strings," like those pictured at right. In each address, the bit string's most significant digits, those to the left, are the row number, and the least significant digits, those to the right, are the column number. The larger the memory, the longer each address has to be. To store data in the computer, the CPU sends the memory a signal containing data, an address, and a "write" command. In response, the memory writes the data to the designated address. Similarly, data is retrieved from memory when the CPU sends memory a "read" signal and an address. The memory goes to the designated address, reads the data there, and sends it to the CPU.

How memory uses addresses

A byte of data is stored at address 001010 of the memory. The address *(bottom left)* sent by the CPU is split into its three most significant bits—001—and the three least significant—010—and put onto the two address buses *(red and blue, below)*. The signals follow set paths and meet at the designated address. There, the write signal opens the address, and the data sent on the data bus *(green)* is stored.

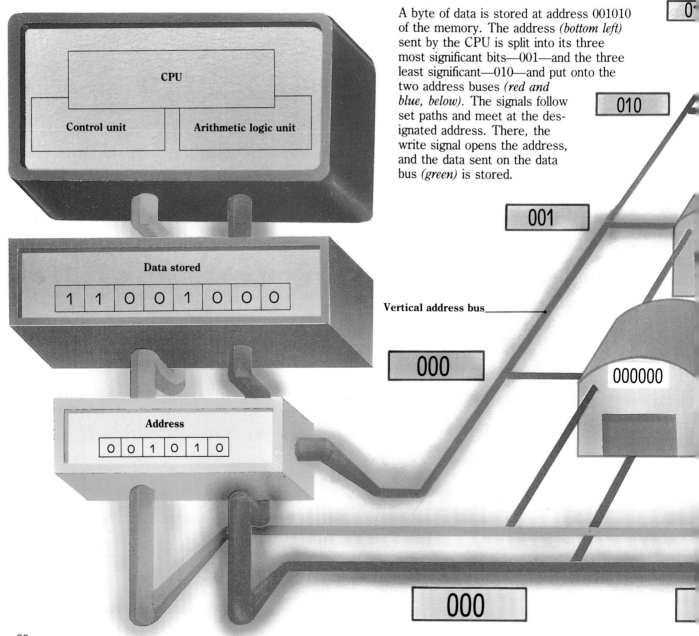

CPU

Control unit

Arithmetic logic unit

Data stored

| 1 | 1 | 0 | 0 | 1 | 0 | 0 | 0 |

Address

| 0 | 0 | 1 | 0 | 1 | 0 |

Vertical address bus

010

001

000

000000

000

A computer's internal memory

The internal memory of a computer is called primary memory to distinguish it from the external memory, where data is stored for future use. Early computers had magnetic primary memory, but now nearly all com-

puters use integrated circuit chips as primary memory. Address buses, or grids of tiny wires, run through each memory unit. These enable the computer to read any piece of data equally fast, no matter where it is stored.

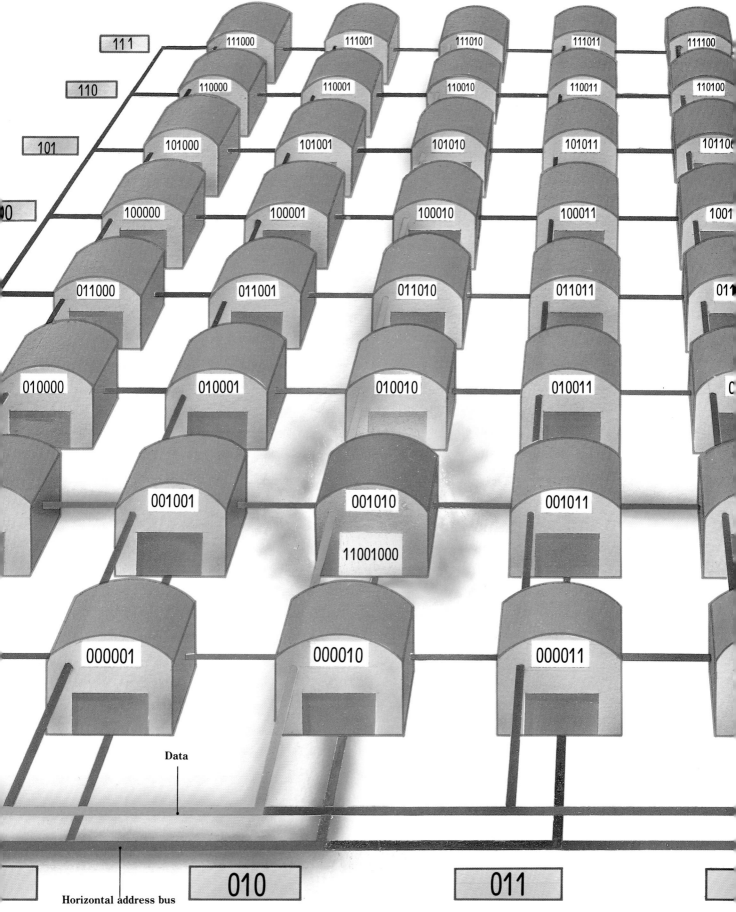

111
111000 111001 111010 111011 111100

110
110000 110001 110010 110011 110100

101
101000 101001 101010 101011 10110(

100000 100001 100010 100011 1001

011000 011001 011010 011011 011

010000 010001 010010 010011

001001 001010 001011

11001000

000001 000010 000011

Data

Horizontal address bus

010   011

31

How Does a Computer Keyboard Work?

In most computer systems, the keyboard is the control panel through which the operator inputs data and tells the computer what to do. Most computer keyboards, like typewriters, have letters and numbers on the keys. When a typewriter key is pressed, however, a hammer with a symbol—the letter A, for example—hits an inked ribbon, printing that symbol on the paper. A computer keyboard is more complex and more versatile: Different symbols or even computer commands can be assigned to each key. A key simply triggers an electronic signal.

Under the keys of most computer keyboards are two sets of wires—horizontal and vertical. When the computer is on, the keyboard's microprocessor sends electrical impulses along the vertical wires, scanning for a signal. When a key is pressed, the wires that cross below it touch

(below), closing a circuit. This alerts the keyboard microprocessor that a key has been pressed; the microprocessor then checks the horizontal wires to see which row the key is in and sends the information to the computer.

Which key has been pressed?

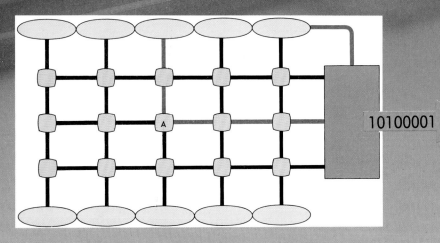

3 **Signaling** the computer. The two wires in contact under the key close a circuit, sending a signal back to the microprocessor *(purple)*. The microprocessor knows which key is pressed because each key activates only one pair of wires. Here, the key is A, and the microprocessor generates its digital code: 10100001.

10100001

A complex device. When a key is pressed *(below, left)*, wires crossing under it send a signal to the keyboard microprocessor. The microprocessor registers the signal and scans for the next; meanwhile, a spring pushes the key back up when it is released.

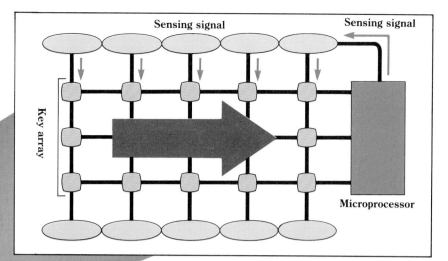

Sensing signal

Sensing signal

Key array

Microprocessor

1 **Ready and scanning.** When the computer is on, the keyboard's microprocessor *(purple)* sends electrical impulses *(small red arrows)* through the vertical wires *(black)* that are beneath the keys *(green)*. It scans from left to right *(large red arrow)* thousands of times each second.

2 **A key is pressed.** The pressed key *(left)* makes the vertical wire touch a horizontal wire, sending the scanning signal along both wires.

Keyboard arrangements and uses

On most computer keyboards, the keys are arranged in the QWERTY layout *(right)*. Named for its top six letter keys and designed for the first typewriters, QWERTY was meant to slow down fast typists so their machines would not jam. Computer keyboards *(below)* have four kinds of keys. Data keys enter letters, numbers, and punctuation marks; shift keys produce capital letters. Cursor control keys move the cursor around on the screen; function keys let the operator issue common commands with just one keystroke.

QWERTY

MALTRON

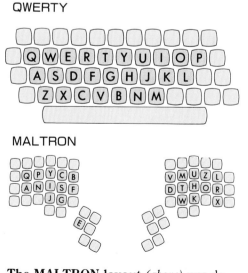

The MALTRON layout *(above)* was designed to boost speed by placing the most-used keys under the fastest fingers.

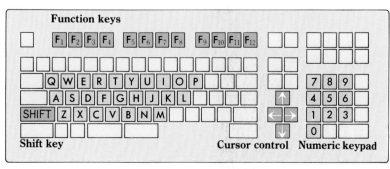

Function keys

F₁ F₂ F₃ F₄   F₅ F₆ F₇ F₈   F₉ F₁₀ F₁₁ F₁₂

Q W E R T Y U I O P

A S D F G H J K L

SHIFT Z X C V B N M

Shift key

7 8 9
4 5 6
1 2 3
0

Cursor control   **Numeric keypad**

33

How Does a Mouse Operate?

The mouse is one of several tools that can be connected to a computer to help the operator move the cursor. The cursor, the blinking rectangle of light on the screen, shows where the operator's next action will occur. When a letter is typed, it appears on the screen in the place marked by the cursor, and the cursor moves one space to the right. The cursor-control keys on the keyboard let the operator move the cursor across the screen or up and down.

But by rolling a mouse on the tabletop *(below)*, the operator can move the cursor around the screen in every direction with the speed of a hand movement. Buttons on the mouse let the operator choose options from an on-screen menu or draw lines on-screen.

There are two kinds of mice, mechanical and optical; each fits easily into the palm of the hand. As the mechanical mouse *(right)* is moved across a desk top, its inner mechanism measures the distance and direction and tells the computer to move the cursor similarly on the monitor. The optical mouse *(below, right)* does this task with light beams, sensing the lines on a grid. A joystick *(opposite, bottom)* serves as the control mechanism for many video games.

Mouse movement and the cursor

Wired electronically to the keyboard, the mouse makes the cursor imitate its movements in both distance and direction. For this reason, the operator must pay attention to the screen while moving the mouse. Since the mouse can be moved in any direction, it can form curved and diagonal lines and is an excellent drawing tool.

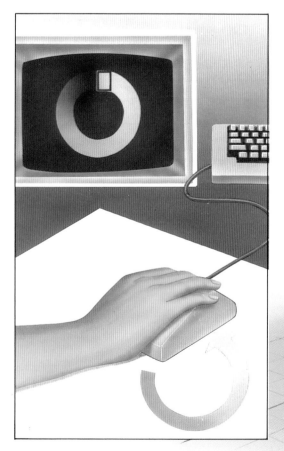

How an optical mouse "sees"

An optical mouse is used on a special grid. As the mouse is moved across the grid, light from an LED, or light-emitting diode, shines onto the grid. A lens and a mirror send the light to a sensor, or photodetector, that notes the number of lines passed.

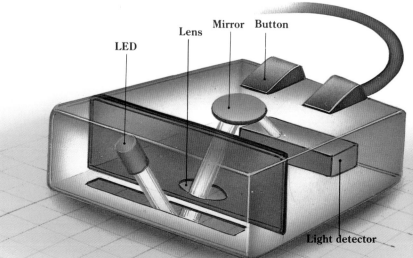

LED   Lens   Mirror   Button

Light detector

How a mechanical mouse works

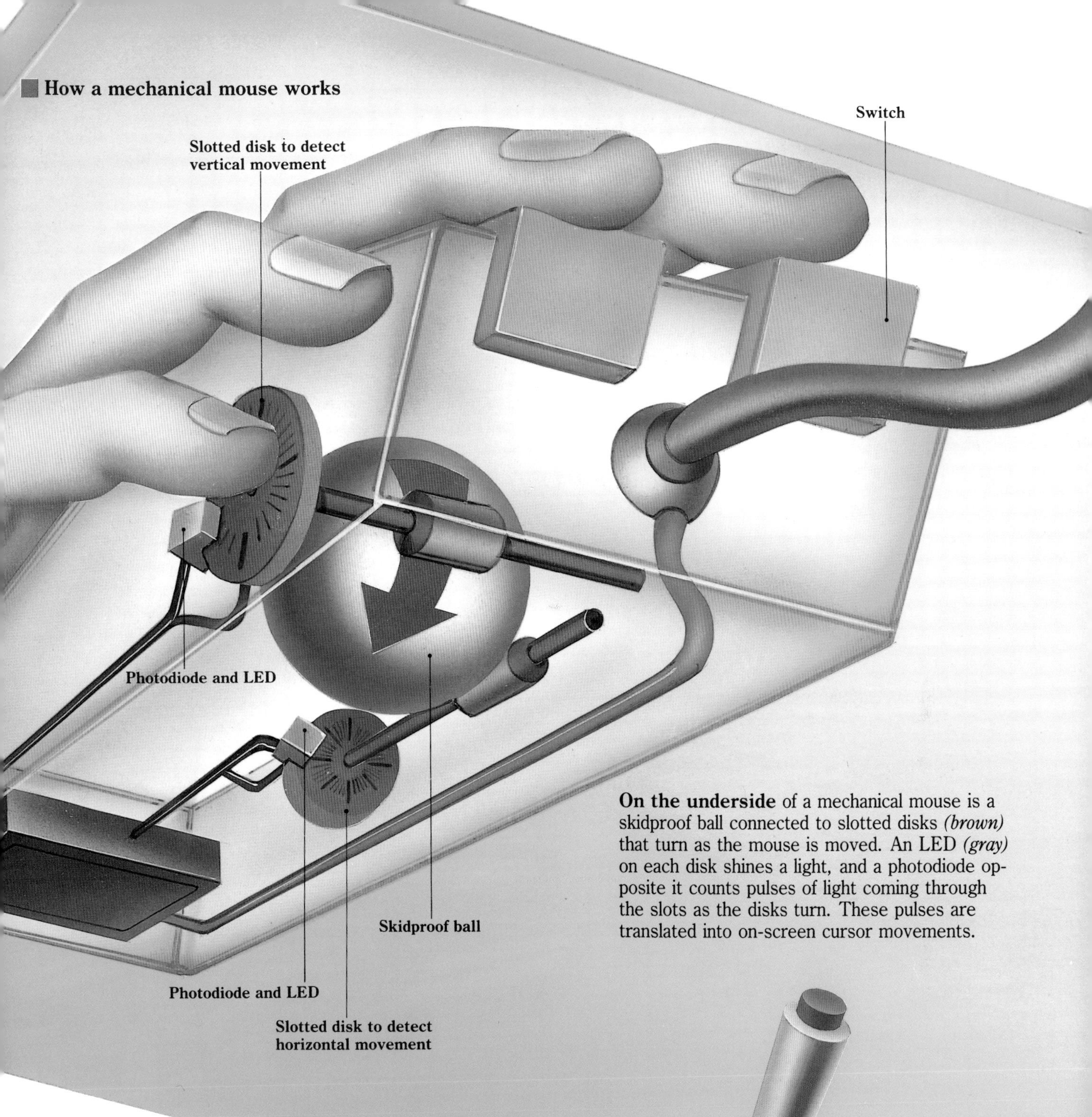

Slotted disk to detect vertical movement

Switch

Photodiode and LED

Skidproof ball

Photodiode and LED

Slotted disk to detect horizontal movement

On the underside of a mechanical mouse is a skidproof ball connected to slotted disks *(brown)* that turn as the mouse is moved. An LED *(gray)* on each disk shines a light, and a photodiode opposite it counts pulses of light coming through the slots as the disks turn. These pulses are translated into on-screen cursor movements.

● Inside a joystick

Like a mouse, a joystick detects motion in two directions and coordinates the signals. The stick fits through a movable shaft *(center)* and into a cradle at a right angle below it *(bottom)*. Two electronic devices called variable resistors send signals that vary with the positions of shaft and cradle and make the cursor move.

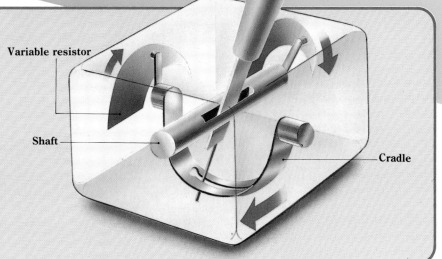

Variable resistor

Shaft

Cradle

How Does Magnetic Storage Work?

To increase their capacity to store information, most computers use magnetic disks or magnetic tape as auxiliary storage. Whether on disks or tape, data is written and read in the form of tiny magnetic charges. A computer's tape drive works like a tape recorder but is wired to the computer. A magnetic hard-disk drive, or fixed drive, is built into many computers.

A hard-disk drive consists of several circular aluminum plates, each coated with magnetic material and each provided with a head that reads and writes data. The whole stack of disks spins, and as it rotates, data can be read or recorded on concentric tracks on the disks' surfaces. Instructed to read or write data, the head moves to the designated track and waits. When the correct sector passes under it, the head reads or writes while the disk keeps turning. The wedge-shaped head floats over the surface of the disk on a cushion of air produced by the disk's high-speed rotation. By emitting rapid magnetic pulses, the head records or erases data on the disk without touching it. Hard disks may have from 200 to 1,000 tracks and may hold from 10 million characters (10 megabytes) to one billion characters (one gigabyte).

Magnetic data storage

One storage method *(top)* uses two magnetic pulses per bit, making north poles face each other for a 1 and face away for a 0. In another method *(bottom)*, when the machine sees a magnetization the same as the one before, it recognizes a 0; if a bit is different from the one preceding it, the machine recognizes it as a 1.

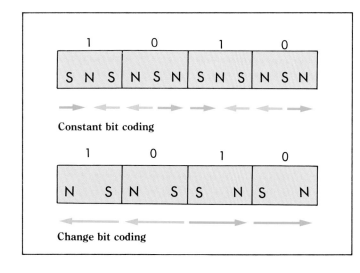

1   0   1   0

S N S | N S N | S N S | N S N

Constant bit coding

1   0   1   0

N | S N | S S | N S | N

Change bit coding

11001010

Anatomy of a hard-disk drive

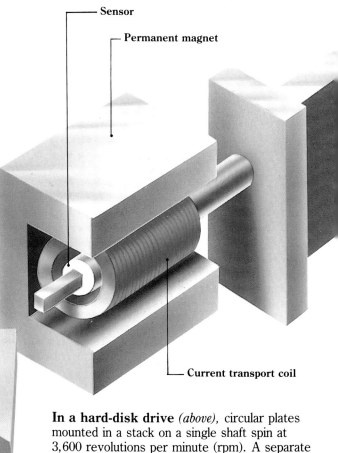

— Sensor

— Permanent magnet

— Current transport coil

In a hard-disk drive *(above)*, circular plates mounted in a stack on a single shaft spin at 3,600 revolutions per minute (rpm). A separate head reaches each of the recording surfaces. Although the access arm moves all the heads over the tracks simultaneously, only one head at a time is instructed to read, write, or erase. Since all disk surfaces are reachable, the heads can read data instantly anywhere on any disk.

Writing to a magnetic disk

When the head writes data on a magnetic disk, bits are recorded in sequence on a track. The diagram above, read from left to right, shows how the head records 1s by using magnetization opposite to that of the previous bit. Zeros are indicated by a bit identical to the preceding one.

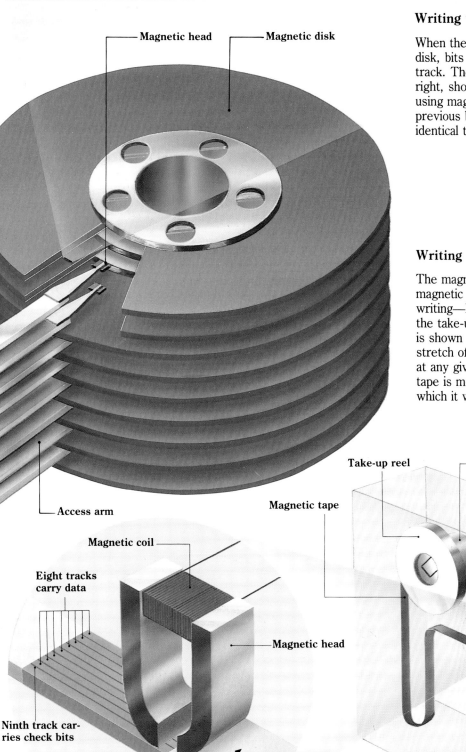

Magnetic head — Magnetic disk

Access arm

Writing to magnetic tape

The magnetic-tape drive *(below)* has three magnetic heads—for erasing, reading, and writing—located between the supply reel and the take-up reel; the write head *(below, left)* is shown here enlarged. Since only a short stretch of the tape is accessible to the heads at any given moment, data that is stored on tape is most easily processed in the order in which it was written.

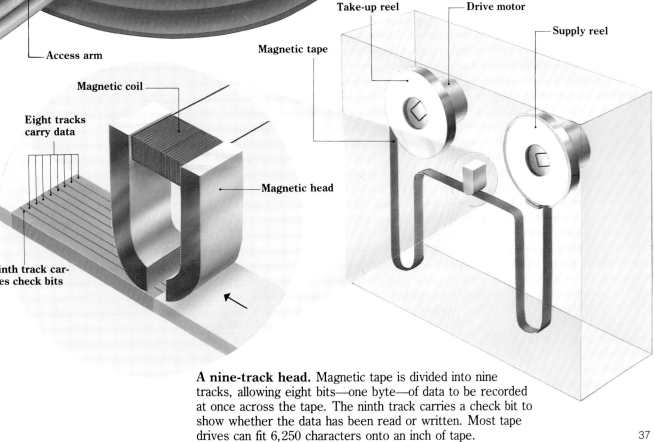

Eight tracks carry data

Magnetic coil

Magnetic head

Ninth track carries check bits

Take-up reel — Drive motor

Magnetic tape

Supply reel

A nine-track head. Magnetic tape is divided into nine tracks, allowing eight bits—one byte—of data to be recorded at once across the tape. The ninth track carries a check bit to show whether the data has been read or written. Most tape drives can fit 6,250 characters onto an inch of tape.

How Does a Printer Work?

A printer is a basic output component, making a permanent copy on paper of data in the computer. Many kinds of printers are available, with different speeds, capabilities, and prices. Some work slowly but produce text as clear as the letters on this page; some make fuzzier printouts very quickly, and others are best for images.

Printers that use hammers—as a typewriter does—to hit an inked ribbon against the paper are called impact printers. Nonimpact printers do not use hammers. An ink-jet printer, for example, shoots tiny drops of ink onto the paper, and a laser printer uses light beams, in the way that a photocopier does. But the most popular printers are impact printers.

Some impact printers, called character printers, print by pressing each character—letter, number, or punctuation mark—against an inked ribbon to make its imprint on the page. Such a machine prints clearly but slowly and can print only the characters installed by the manufacturer. Another kind of impact printer, the dot-matrix printer, is the kind used in most homes and offices. It is comparatively fast and inexpensive. Instead of characters, it hammers in a set of small pins *(right)*, each of which can print a dot. A character is formed when a selection of pins is pressed against the inked ribbon as the printhead moves across the paper. Not only can these rapid-firing pins print up to 300 characters per second, but they also can be used to make characters in several languages and for graphics.

How a dot-matrix printer works

A dot-matrix impact printer

An inked ribbon runs between the paper and the printhead; the printhead moves across the paper, printing as it goes. When the printhead has filled a line, the paper-feed motor turns the platen to move the paper up one line.

Paper-feed motor

Printhead

Inked ribbon

Platen

Pins in a line. The pins of the printhead strike the inked ribbon, printing dots onto the paper behind it. The printhead fires only those pins needed to make the required pattern.

Pins

Printhead

Inside the printhead. The printhead has seven pins in a vertical row, each attached to its hammer. The pins are fired at the paper and retracted hundreds of times per second by electromagnets. The printhead moves the width of one dot at a time and must print five times to produce one letter.

Holding data in the buffer

A computer can send data much faster than a printer can print it. For this reason, the printer is equipped with a memory, called a buffer, where data is stored until it can be printed. The buffer increases printer speed by letting it print in both directions. That is, after printing a line from left to right, the printhead prints the next line from right to left rather than first returning to the left margin.

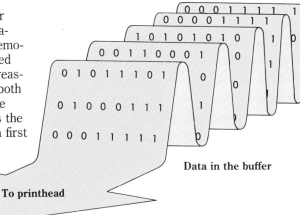

Data in the buffer

To printhead

How Is Analog Data Digitized?

The world is full of measurable quantities. Some quantities change gradually, and some change step by step. That is to say, such things as temperature and the loudness of a sound show no clear division between one value and the next. Quantities that change in this continuous, or stepless, manner are said to be analog values. In contrast, an electrical switch is either on or off, with nothing in-between; if a telephone number is 123-4567, then the next one is 123-4568, with nothing in-between. Quantities that progress in this step-by-step fashion are called digital values.

The circuits inside a computer are digital and operate on the basis of a pair of electrical conditions: on/off or high/low voltage. There are no in-between values. These two conditions correspond to the numerical values 1 and 0, so that all arithmetic values can be represented in terms of this binary system. The binary digits 1 and 0 can also be used in combinations to represent other symbols, such as letters of the alphabet. Before information can be put into a computer, it must be represented in binary digital values—1s and 0s. Pressing a letter key on the computer's keyboard *(page 32)* triggers a train of 1s and 0s that represent that letter.

Analog values, on the other hand, cannot be input directly to the computer, nor can the computer output them. They must first be processed by an analog/digital (A/D) converter. For example, a musical tone *(below, left)* picked up by a microphone is first converted from sound waves into an analog voltage. Then the A/D converter produces a series of digital values closely corresponding to the original, and this is input to the computer. To produce an output, the computer's digital signal is D/A converted—changed from digital to analog. This conversion technology allows the computer to receive data from both the digital and the analog worlds.

Data I/O and the computer

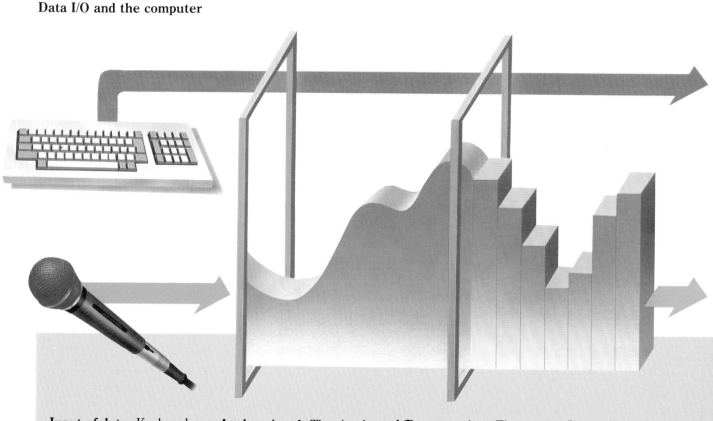

Input of data. Keyboard signals are input; the voice from a microphone is not.

Analog signal. The signal from the microphone produces a smooth wave-form.

A/D conversion. The wave is changed into steps of corresponding heights.

Input. The information, now in digital form, is fed into the computer.

Analog and digital conversion

To convert analog quantities to digital, the analog wave-form for a given time period—for example, one second of a song—must be divided into short, equal segments. Then the height of the wave-form in each segment is expressed as a numerical value. Thus the analog quantity becomes a series of numerical values, one for each segment. The numerical values can be represented by the computer's electrical signals.

Conversely, to convert a digital quantity to an analog, the series of numerical values is first converted into a corresponding voltage for each segment in order. Then these separate heights are joined by a smoothly curving wave.

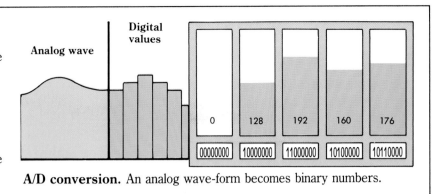

A/D conversion. An analog wave-form becomes binary numbers.

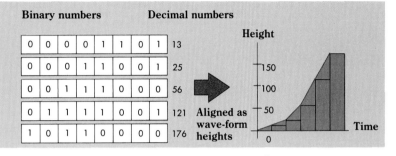

D/A conversion. Binary numbers become an analog wave.

Information in digital form, such as that produced by keys pressed on the keyboard *(below, left),* can go directly into the computer. But information that is in analog form, such as the sound of a voice, must be converted to digital form before being input. Similarly, computer output *(below)* is only in digital form; to obtain analog information, such as music, D/A conversion must occur.

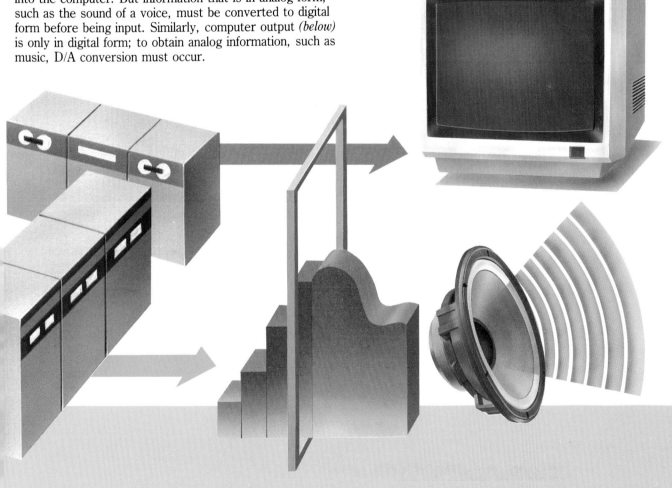

Digital output. The computer puts out its result as a digital signal.

D/A conversion. The digital signal is changed to an analog signal.

Analog output. The data emerges on a monitor or as sound from a speaker.

What Is a Supercomputer?

Some problems are too complex even for mainframe computers. Mapping the wind patterns in a storm or the water flow around one rock in a rushing creek would take scientists a long time on a mainframe. Similarly, very large numbers in astronomy are too unwieldy for standard computers to handle. Supercomputers have no trouble with huge numbers and are equipped to handle many equations simultaneously, performing billions of calculations in a second.

This great speed has been achieved in several ways. By making circuits more and more compact, engineers have shortened the distance each electrical impulse has to travel inside the computer. Chemists have developed a synthetic semiconductor, gallium arsenide, that conducts electricity faster than silicon can. And designers have built arrays of many microprocessors, linked to handle data in new ways.

A traditional computer works sequentially: It reads a command, calculates the data address, and executes each command before starting to read the next. But multiple microprocessors within a supercomputer carry out these tasks in an overlapping manner, called parallel or pipeline processing, letting the computer process many commands at one time. And by arranging data into vectors, or arrays, supercomputers can process long lists of numbers simultaneously.

Two approaches to processing

Sequential processing

Raw material (data)

Pipeline processing

Raw material (data)

Shaping sides

Packing the pipeline. The top dice-making assembly line represents sequential processing, in which one microprocessor handles only one piece of data at a time and finishes it before starting a new one. In pipeline processing *(red boxes, bottom),* four microprocessors handle data, starting on new items before others are done and turning work out four times as fast.

The Cray Y-MP. Built in 1988, this modern super-computer features eight microprocessors, each with 14 pipeline operators. Its components are arranged in a C-shape, rather than in a row, to shorten the distances impulses must travel, and it can complete more than two billion calculations per second.

Finished product
(processed data)

Finished product
(processed data)

Painting dots on dice

Shaping front and back

Shaping top
and bottom

Leaps and bounds. Although these computers handle data somewhat differently, this graph gives a rough comparison of their speed. Each space equals 10 times as many operations as the one to its left.

Operations per second of four kinds of computers

	10^5	10^6	10^7	10^8	10^9	10^{10}
Supercomputer						
Mainframe						
Minicomputer						
Personal computer (16-bit)						

Vector processing for speed

Some scientific data can be organized into special lists, or arrays, called vectors. Two vectors can be added *(right),* yielding a new vector of their sums *(far right).* To gain computing speed, a vector processor handles each item as a process element and adds all the sums at once, as fast as it would add two numbers.

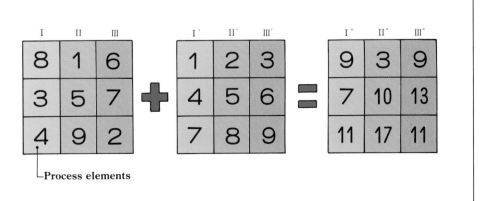

Process elements

43

What Is a Neurocomputer?

A neurocomputer is designed to imitate the structure and functioning of the human brain. Although any computer can outcalculate people, a biological brain has two traits that enable it to work more efficiently than computers on certain kinds of problems. It can make decisions, even when the data is incomplete, and it can learn.

Scientists are developing computers that may accomplish these two human feats by building them to resemble the human brain. After all, some researchers say, the brain, like the computer, is a processor of electrical impulses. The brain is built up of billions of specialized cells in which impulses are processed in the cell body, or neuron, and travel along the axon.

One kind of neurocomputer is illustrated below. It consists of three layers *(blue grids)* of neuronlike cells, joined by thousands of axonlike connections. These connections are random and equally weak when the system is first built. But they are selectively strengthened as the computer is taught to accomplish a task in the same way that electrical impulses in the brain forge pathways where human learning is stored.

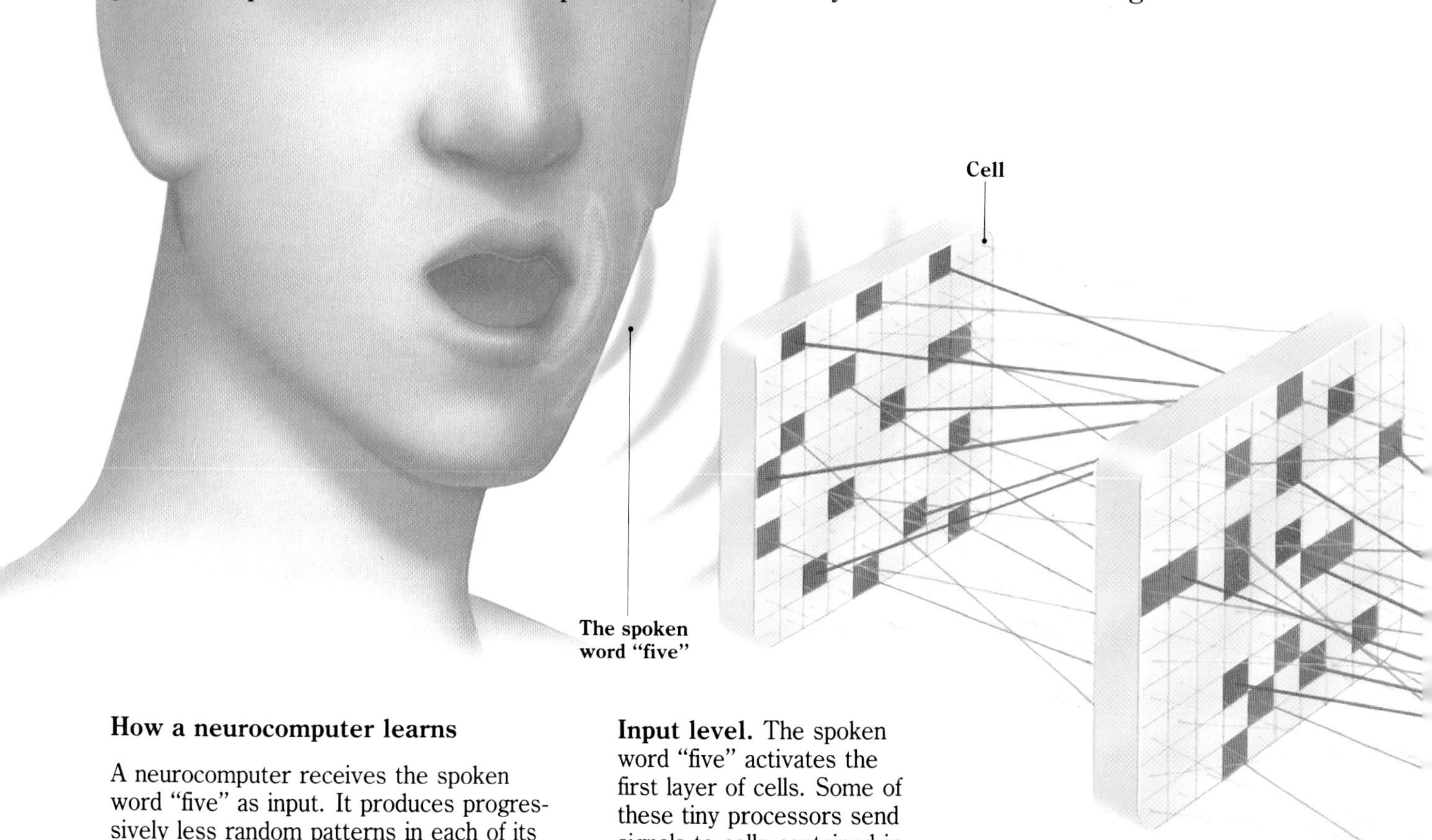

Cell

The spoken word "five"

How a neurocomputer learns

A neurocomputer receives the spoken word "five" as input. It produces progressively less random patterns in each of its three layers of simulated neurons and generates a rough version of the symbol 5. With training, it eventually will produce a precise image *(opposite, bottom)*.

Input level. The spoken word "five" activates the first layer of cells. Some of these tiny processors send signals to cells contained in the next layer.

Intermediate layer. Cells in the next layer pick up the input signals and evaluate them. Some send signals to cells in the third, or output, layer.

Learning connections

At first all neurocomputer circuits are equally weak *(right)*, but a correct response establishes a few strong connections *(far right)* in the network, and the computer can be said to have learned. Used repeatedly, the learned task becomes memory.

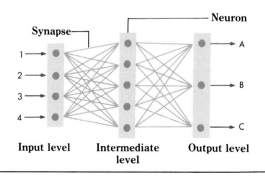

Neural network before learning

Synapse

Neuron

1 →
2 →
3 →
4 →

A

B

C

Input level   Intermediate level   Output level

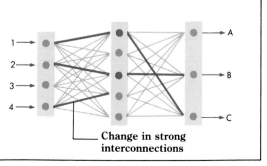

Neural network after learning

1 →
2 →
3 →
4 →

A

B

C

Change in strong interconnections

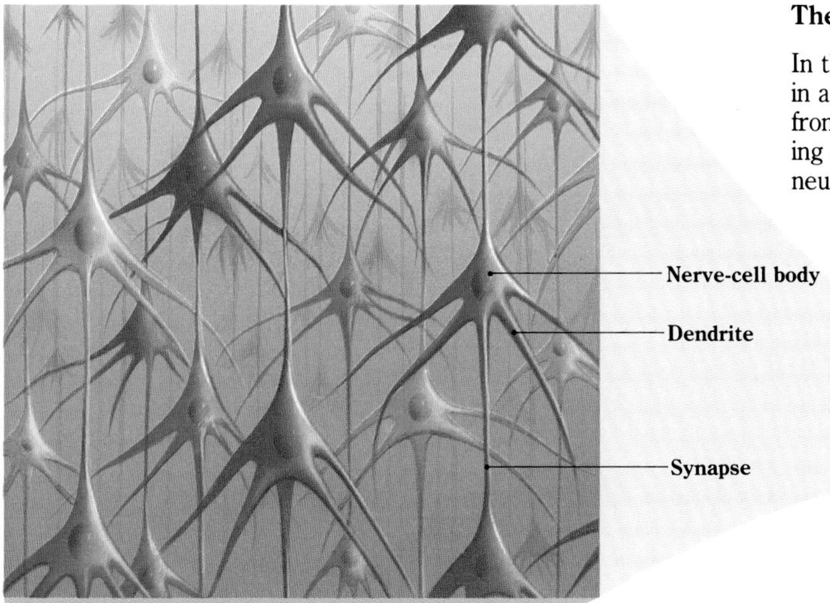

The neurons of the human brain

In the human brain, billions of nerve cells are joined in a dense network *(left)*. Electrical impulses travel from cell to cell across synapses *(below)*, establishing new pathways with each new bit of learning. A neurocomputer is built to imitate these cells.

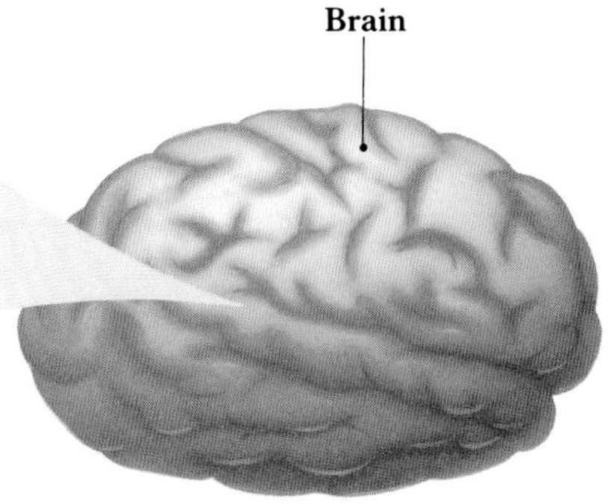

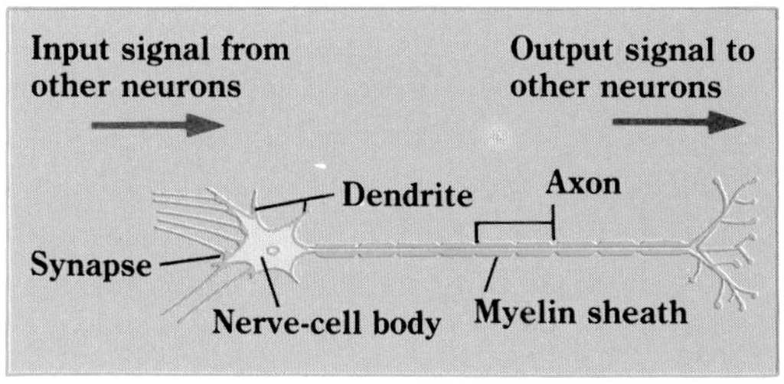

Nerve-cell body

Dendrite

Synapse

Brain

Input signal from other neurons

Output signal to other neurons

Dendrite

Axon

Synapse

Nerve-cell body

Myelin sheath

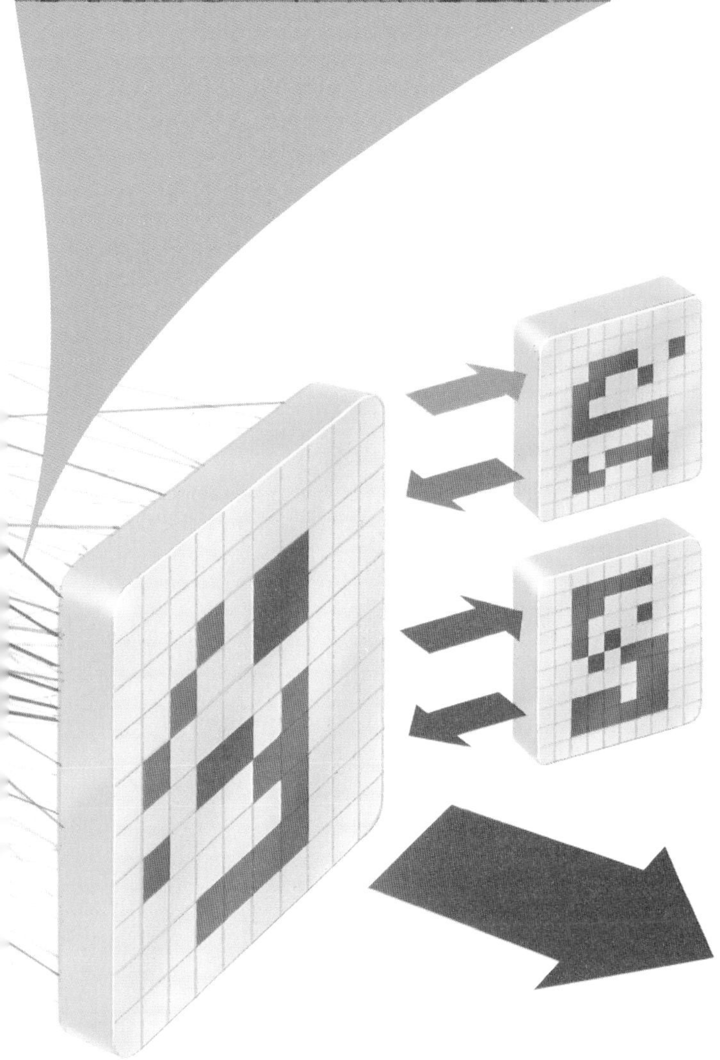

Learning through feedback. For each acceptable output, the technician tells the machine to retain the connections that produced it. In this way, the circuits that contribute parts of the correct pattern are strengthened, and those that lie outside the pattern area gradually weaken.

The desired response to a spoken "five"

Output layer. An incomplete but acceptable pattern *(above)* emerges. The technician training the neurocomputer instructs the machine to retain the connections that produced the image. The next time the neurocomputer hears this sound, it will produce a better pattern.

3

Software

People often say, "Computers have done this," or, "Computers have done that." In fact, computers do nothing at all except what human beings tell them to do. Computers are simply machines carrying out instructions that people give them. Those instructions, or commands, which tell computers to execute a series of specific tasks, are known as programs. Collectively, programs, along with the disks or tapes on which they are stored, are known as software. The physical components of the computer are called the hardware. By itself, hardware cannot do anything. Combined with software, computers are capable of carrying out a wide variety of tasks, from playing a game of tick-tack-toe to running a nation's banking system. The capabilities of computers are limited only by the skill, ingenuity, and imagination of the people who design and write the software. Each problem must first be broken down into several algorithms, or carefully defined problems, to be solved. The algorithms are then translated into a computer language, such as FORTRAN, COBOL, or BASIC. These languages serve as the link between the 0s and 1s of binary digits (or bits) that computers can understand and the more complex languages used by humans.

The software is the brain of a computer. It defines the instructions the computer is to carry out. Until a program has been loaded into the computer's memory, the computer is like a body without a brain, unable to perform any actions.

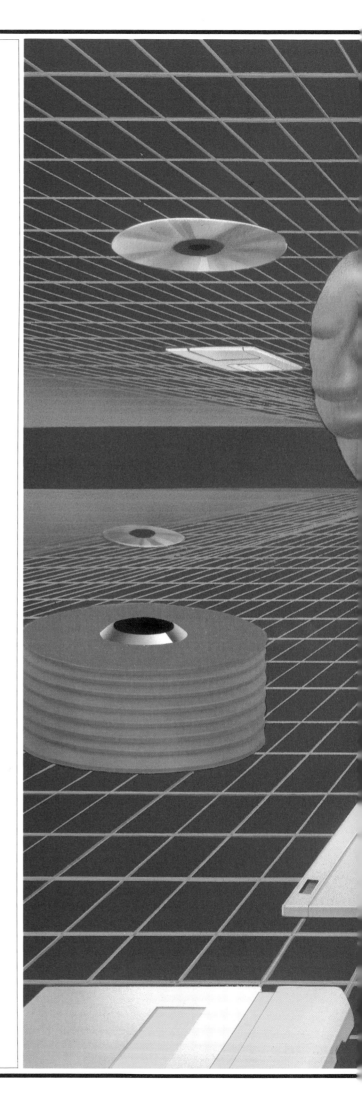

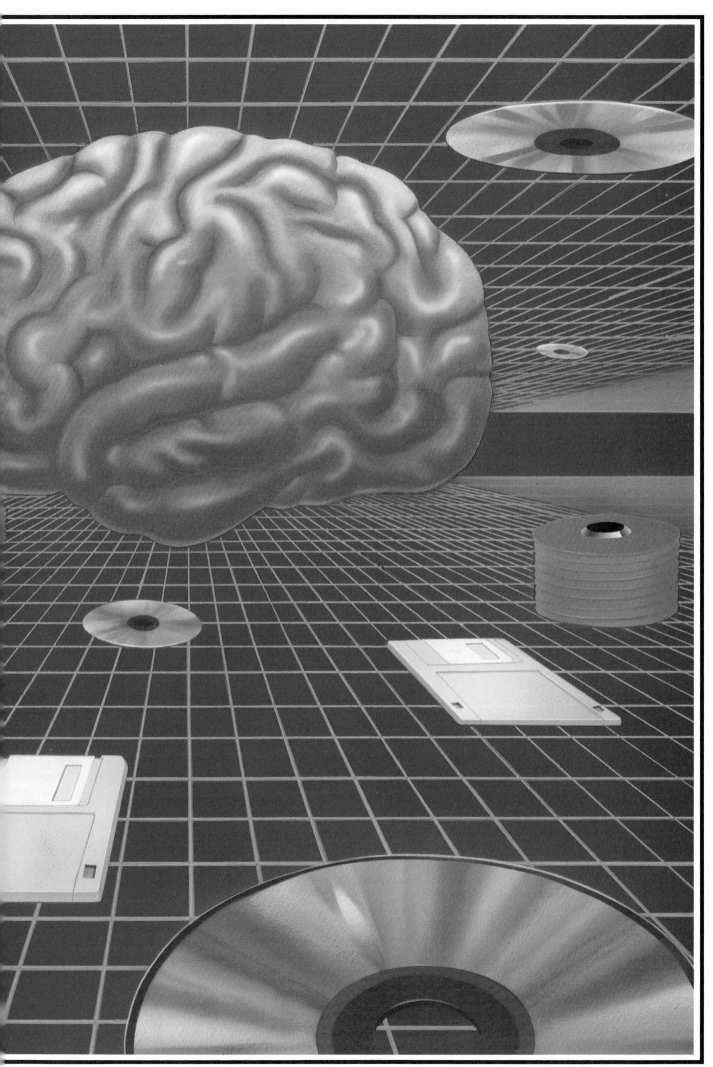

What Is a Computer Program?

A program functions as the script of a play in which the computer is an actor. The program tells the computer exactly what to do and say in each act of the production. Once a program is loaded into the computer's memory, the play can begin. The computer reads the program line by line; decodes, or translates, the program's commands into 0s and 1s; then carries out the instructions. A program consists of many simple commands, such as "Accept data from the keyboard" or "Decide which of two numbers is larger." A combination of these simple tasks written in a program instructs the computer to perform more complex and sophisticated actions. Programs with internal housekeeping functions, such as adding numbers and sorting files, are known as utility programs. The large programs that are familiar to most people—such as word processors, spreadsheets, and games—are known as applications software. As a computer does only what it is told to do, programs must be carefully constructed to avoid what is known as GIGO—"Garbage In, Garbage Out."

The role of the program

A computer loads a program by storing it in its memory. Then each command is called up in sequence and decoded by the controller. Electrical signals are sent out by the controller instructing various devices to perform specified tasks. For example, if the first command refers to a keyboard entry, a signal is relayed to the keyboard allowing it to accept input from the operator. When the data has been entered, it is stored, and the computer moves to the next command in the program.

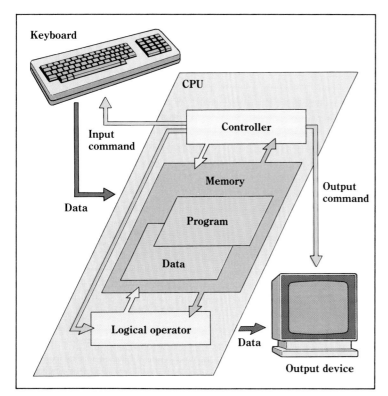

Keyboard

CPU

Input command

Data

Controller

Memory

Output command

Program

Data

Logical operator

Data

Output device

Writing a program

A program has several distinct phases. Here, a program in the BASIC language instructs a computer to display an oval on the cathode-ray tube, or CRT, screen.

2 Writing. The programmer writes the commands in an orderly sequence, following the rules of syntax of the programming language that is used.

```
10   CLS
20   CIRCLE (320, 200), 190, 1, , ,1
30   END
```

3 Testing. The programmer runs the program to see if everything is correct. If data is required, the programmer must provide both correct data and random data to check the accuracy of the entire program. In the program above, line 20 instructs the computer to draw a circle with its center at 320 pixels across and 200 pixels down. The length of the circle's radius is defined by 190, and the arc by 1,,,1.

1 Analyzing. The programmer determines what steps must be taken to produce the desired result and in what order.

● Modifying a program

Once a program is written, it can be modified to perform additional tasks by inserting a few more commands, as below: to draw concentric circles, to draw a few ovals inside a circle, and to draw many ovals.

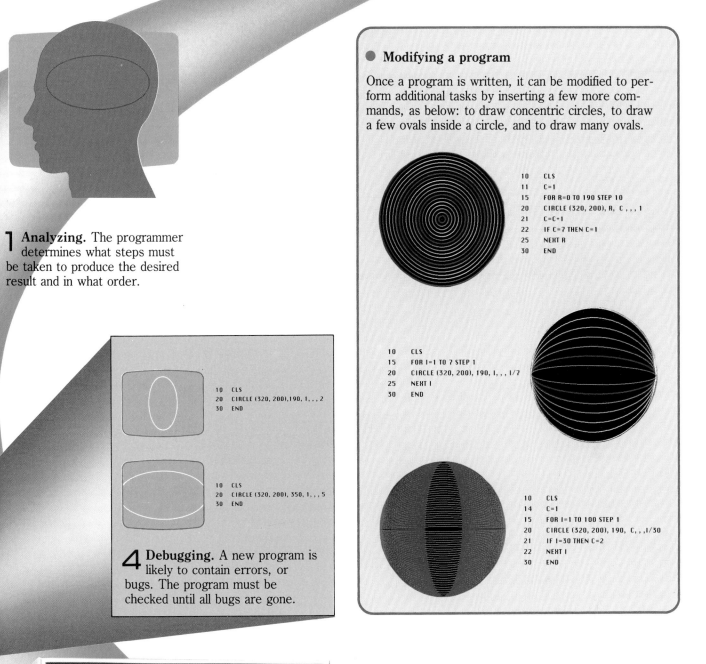

```
10   CLS
11   C=1
15   FOR R=0 TO 190 STEP 10
20   CIRCLE (320, 200), R, C , , , 1
21   C=C+1
22   IF C=7 THEN C=1
25   NEHT R
30   END
```

```
10   CLS
15   FOR I=1 TO 7 STEP 1
20   CIRCLE (320, 200), 190, I, , , 1/7
25   NEHT I
30   END
```

```
10   CLS
14   C=1
15   FOR I=1 TO 100 STEP 1
20   CIRCLE (320, 200), 190, C, , ,1/30
21   IF I=30 THEN C=2
22   NEHT I
30   END
```

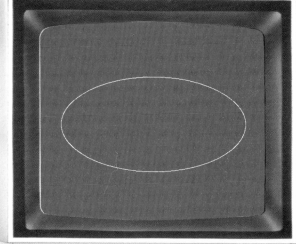

```
10   CLS
20   CIRCLE (320, 200),190, 1, , , 2
30   END
```

```
10   CLS
20   CIRCLE (320, 200), 350, 1, , , 5
30   END
```

4 Debugging. A new program is likely to contain errors, or bugs. The program must be checked until all bugs are gone.

5 Saving. When the program is completely debugged and running correctly, the programmer saves, or moves, it to a storage medium, such as a disk, so that it can be used whenever it is needed.

```
10   CLS
20   CIRCLE (320, 200), 190, 1, , , 5
30   END
```

What Languages Do Computers Use?

At the most basic level, computers cannot understand anything but binary digits—0s and 1s. In this machine language, everything is expressed in the simplest possible terms: 0 or 1, on or off, yes or no. But it is difficult for people to express themselves solely in these terms, so computer programs are written in any of several programming languages. The computer translates instructions coded in programming language into understandable machine language. Many different types of programming languages have been developed. Some, called assembly languages, are easy to translate into machine language. More complex programming languages, in which a single word may signify an entire group of machine language instructions, are known as compiler languages. Part of the art of programming lies in selecting a high-level language—a language that approximates human language closely—that is appropriate to the task at hand. High-level languages have been developed for specific applications, such as business processing, scientific and technical calculations, games, graphics, simulations, and artificial intelligence.

Linking humans with computers

Three programming languages

FORTRAN

COBOL

BASIC

Programming languages make it easier for humans to write instructions for computers. They also allow the same program to be used on many different types of machines. Three of the programming languages are BASIC, which was developed for instructional purposes; COBOL, often used in business processing; and FORTRAN, designed specifically for calculations involving science and technology.

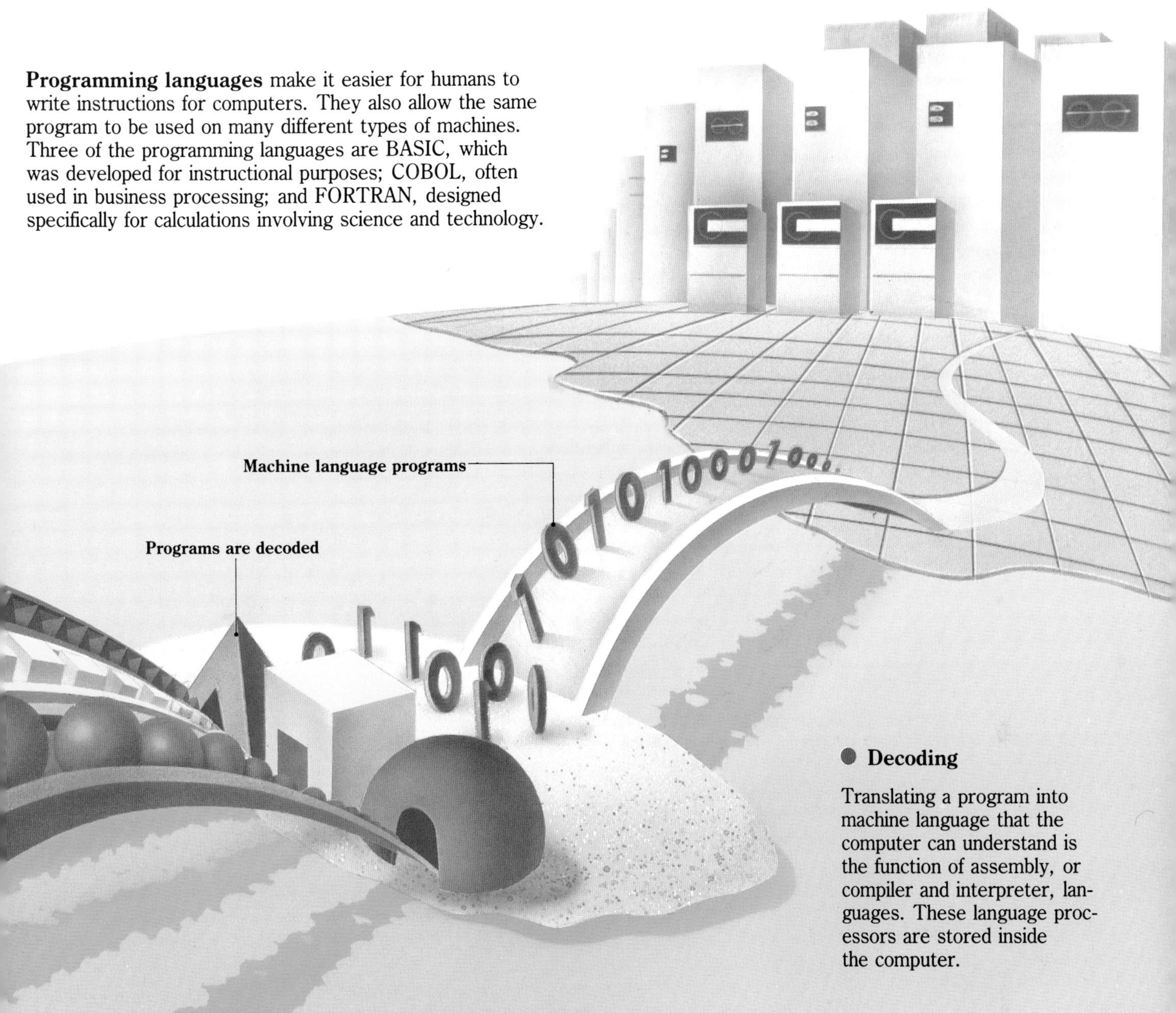

Machine language programs

Programs are decoded

● **Decoding**

Translating a program into machine language that the computer can understand is the function of assembly, or compiler and interpreter, languages. These language processors are stored inside the computer.

Programs in three languages

All three programs shown here ask for two numbers to be entered; the program calls them A and B. The numbers will then be added together and the printer will print out the result; in other words, A+B=C. The form of these commands differs depending on which programming language is used.

```
10   PRINT "A+B=?"
20   INPUT "A=";A
30   INPUT "B=";B
40   C=A+B
50   PRINT A; "=";B"=";C
60   END
```

A BASIC program

```
PROCEDURE DIVISION
P-START.
      OPEN INPUT CARD-FILE.
      OPEN OUTPUT PRINT-FILE.
COMPUTING-RTN.
      READ CARD-FILE AT END GO TO P-TERMINATE.
      COMPUTE C-VAL = A-VAL + B-VAL.
      WRITE PRINT-RECORD AFTER 2 LINES.
      GO TO COMPUTING-RTN.
P-TERMINATE. CLOSE CARD-FILE, PRINT-FILE.
      STOP RUN.
```

A COBOL program

```
         WRITE (6,100)
100   FORMAT (5H A+B )
         READ (5,200) IA, IB
200   FORMAT (I5, I5)
         ISUM = IA + IB
         WRITE (6,101) ISUB
101   FORMAT (1H=, I6)
         STOP
         END
```

A FORTRAN program

What Is an Algorithm?

An algorithm is a carefully defined, finite set of rules and instructions for solving a specific problem. For example, an algorithm for taking a morning shower would include instructions, such as "Take off clothes," "Get into shower," "Wash," "Get out of shower," "Dry off," and "Put clothes back on." Note that these instructions must be followed in the correct order if the shower problem is to be solved successfully. Other morning activities, such as "Brush your teeth," are irrelevant to the specific problem of taking a shower and should not be included.

Computer programs must be precise and concise. Instructions must follow in the proper sequence and should not include unnecessary steps. A badly written algorithm may succeed in solving a problem, but a more elegant algorithm may solve it in fewer steps, thus reducing the time required for processing by the computer. To ensure that their algorithms are correct, logical, and concise, programmers devise simple line drawings known as flow charts, which allow complex problems to be broken down into a series of manageable, easy-to-visualize steps.

Algorithm to repaint balls and mark those that weigh less

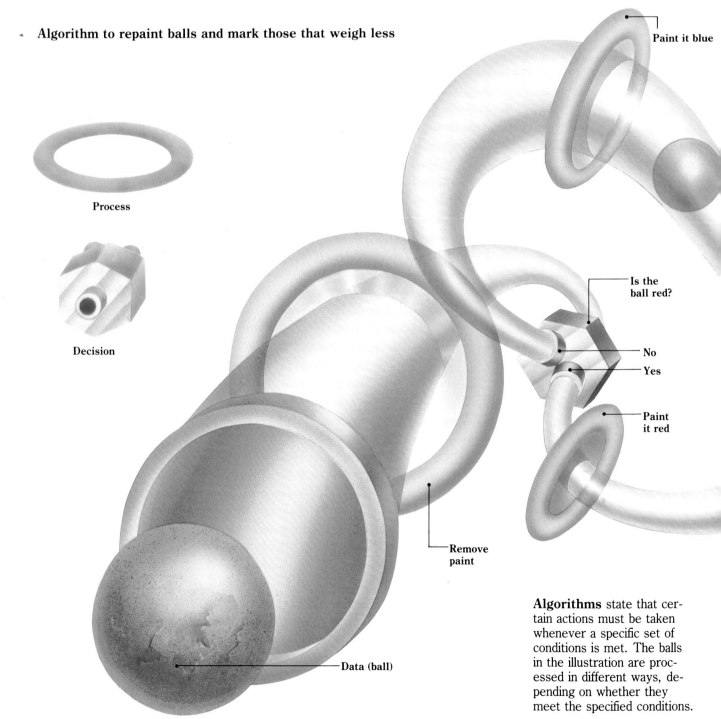

Process

Decision

Paint it blue

Is the ball red?

No

Yes

Paint it red

Remove paint

Data (ball)

Algorithms state that certain actions must be taken whenever a specific set of conditions is met. The balls in the illustration are processed in different ways, depending on whether they meet the specified conditions.

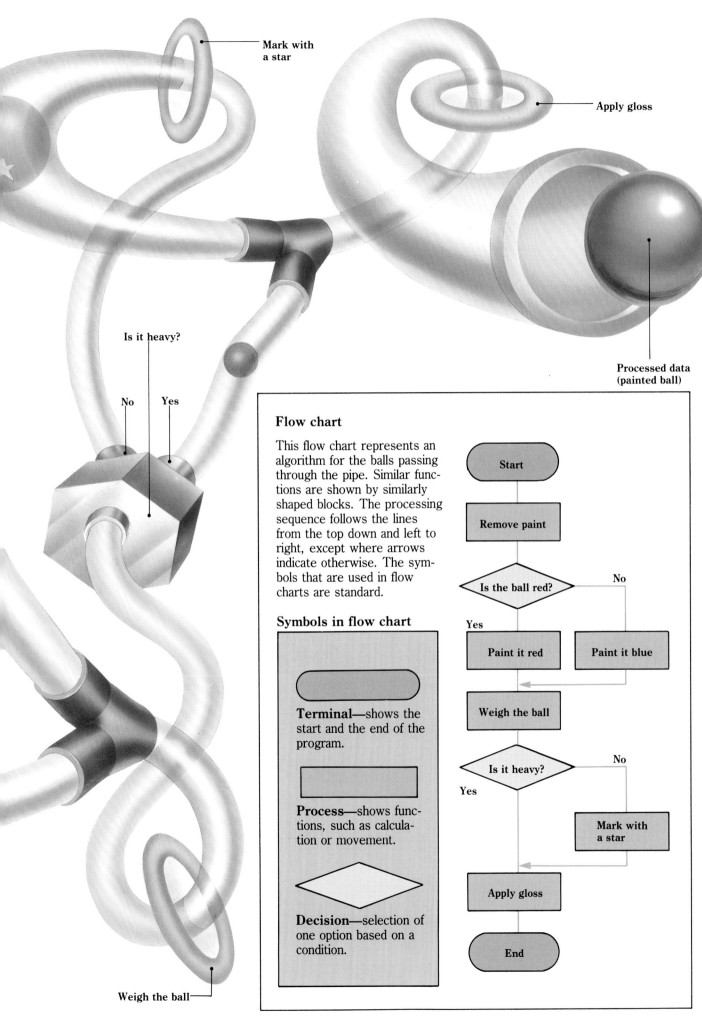

Mark with
a star

Apply gloss

Is it heavy?

No   Yes

Processed data
(painted ball)

Flow chart

This flow chart represents an algorithm for the balls passing through the pipe. Similar functions are shown by similarly shaped blocks. The processing sequence follows the lines from the top down and left to right, except where arrows indicate otherwise. The symbols that are used in flow charts are standard.

Symbols in flow chart

Terminal—shows the start and the end of the program.

Process—shows functions, such as calculation or movement.

Decision—selection of one option based on a condition.

Start

Remove paint

Is the ball red?   No

Yes

Paint it red   Paint it blue

Weigh the ball

Is it heavy?   No

Yes

Mark with
a star

Apply gloss

End

Weigh the ball

How Does a Computer Sort Information?

Sorting information is one of the most important operations a computer performs. By sorting, the computer is able to arrange similar data items in a particular order, be it numerical, alphabetical, or some other sequence. On command, the computer can compare any two of those data items and determine which is the next one in that sequence. In a string of data in random order, the first two items are called up and compared and their relative places in the sequence determined.

The one that is next in the sequence is then compared with a third item, and so on, until the last item in the entire sequence is identified. Then the second item in line is found by the same process. When there are no data items left, the entire sequence will have been sorted in ascending order. This process is known as a bubble sort, because some of the items that are being sorted rise through the list like bubbles moving upward through a liquid.

Sorting information

Because sorting is such a common activity, computers often have a built-in capability to sort various types of data. The operator can specify how the data is to be sorted and whether it should be in ascending or descending order.

Unsorted records

Files and records

A collection of similar data items is known as a file, and each item is a record. In a file on students, for example, each record contains items about each student, such as student number, name, or date of birth. Sorting can be done according to any type of information in the record.

Storage of sorted data

Once data has been sorted, it is stored internally or on a magnetic disk or tape and can be printed out on paper *(below)*. The stored data can then be used in subsequent processing operations.

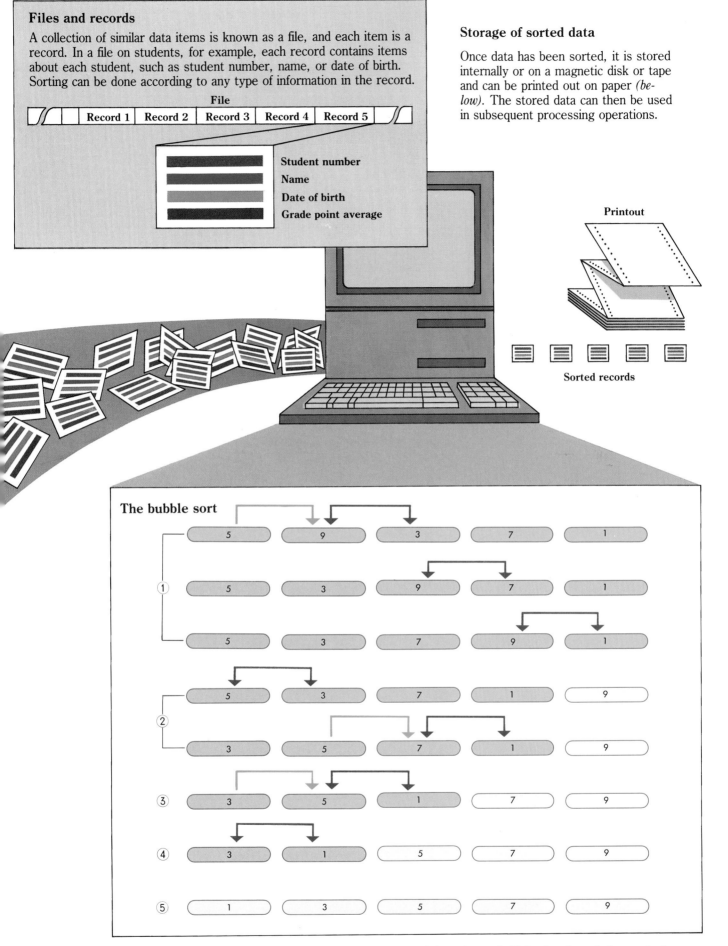

Bubble sorting lets the computer arrange data items in ascending order. Pairs of data items are compared in numerical sequence here. If the first item in a pair is smaller *(blue arrow)*, the items are left unchanged. If the first item is larger *(red arrow)*, their positions are reversed. The comparisons continue in steps 1-4, until all items are arranged in the proper sequence, as in step 5.

How Does a Computer Find Information?

A computer's memory contains information stored as a stream of data. The information can be logically organized into files with separate records within files and individual items within records. When files are arranged this way in a database, each record contains identification labels known as keys. A key could be a code number, or perhaps a name or a date. When seeking a particular record, the computer calls up each item sequentially or directly, depending on the computer storage, and checks to see if it contains the proper key. If the data is stored on tape, each file is said to have sequential organization; if the data is stored on a disk or a hard drive, the data can be accessed sequentially or directly.

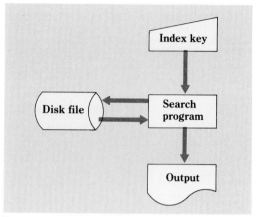

Basic information search program. When a key is entered for a record, the computer scans its memory and displays that record.

Searching for information

● Data storage on magnetic disks

The track of a magnetic disk stores not only data but also addresses for the data, which make it easier for the computer to access information directly. In the call-out below, the disk address is recorded in the count area, and the contents of the key items are stored in the key area.

Count

Key

Data record

The search program goes to work as soon as the key is entered. In files with direct organization, the search program calculates the data's address from the key, retrieves the information, and tells the operating system to read out the data.

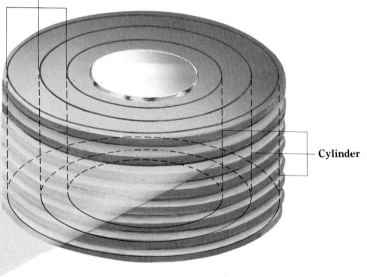

Hard disks and addresses

Track

Cylinder

FLOWERING PLANTS

1. SPECIES
2. VARIETIES
3. PLANTING   7. PREVIOUS PAGE
4. PROPAGATION
5. FERTILIZERS   8. NEXT PAGE
6. PESTS   9. END

An information search screen allows the operator to obtain information simply by selecting an item from a menu rather than by directly entering a key.

A hard disk is made up of several circular plates stacked on a single shaft. A cylinder consists of all the tracks that occupy the same position on each of the plates. The cylinders are numbered from the outside in, and the tracks of each cylinder are numbered from the top down. Thus, the address of a particular data item would be cylinder xx, track yy.

How searches are conducted

1. Sequential search. The computer scans for data in order, starting from the head. The larger the amount of data, the poorer the efficiency of this method.
2. Direct search. The location of the desired data is found from the key. The data must therefore be stored in a particular location relative to the key.
3. Binary search. Data must be arranged in the order of the keys. The middle data item is always checked first to determine whether the desired data is at a higher or lower key. This cuts in half the range to be searched each time an item is checked.

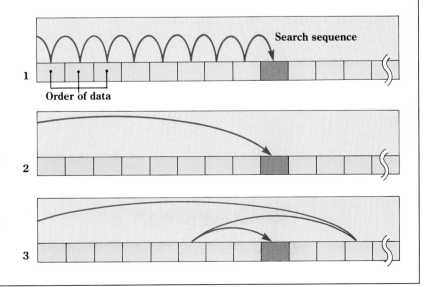

Search sequence

Order of data

1

2

3

What Is a Word Processor?

The keyboard of a computer looks just like the keyboard of a typewriter but with a few extra keys. One of the most common uses of computers today is as a word processor—basically, a sophisticated typewriter that is capable of storing and manipulating text. With a few keystrokes, a writer can insert or delete words and move entire sentences or paragraphs from one place to another in the text. This capability has revolutionized the age-old process of writing and editing, making it possible to revise manuscripts with speed and ease. Writers and editors can tinker with text until they are satisfied, then simply print out clean, error-free hard copy. Entire books can be written, shipped, edited, and printed with the use of computer disks without ever being committed to paper.

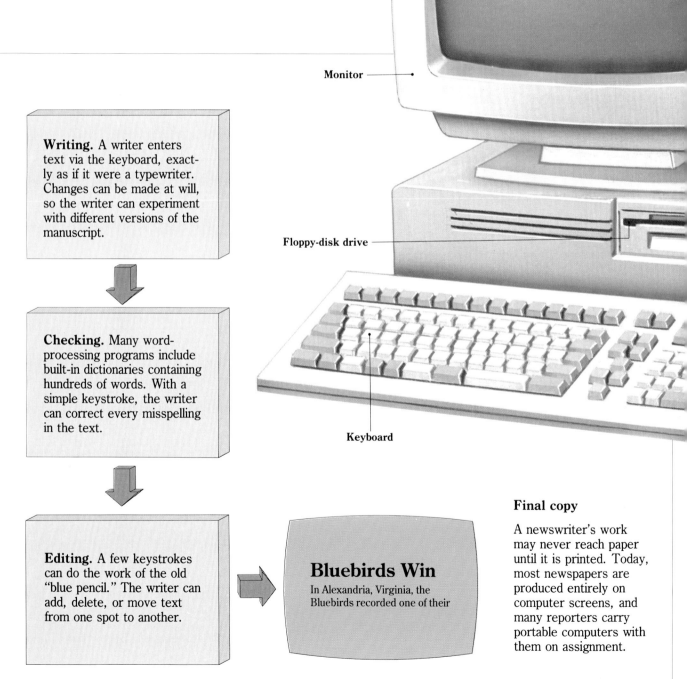

Personal computer

Monitor

Floppy-disk drive

Keyboard

Writing. A writer enters text via the keyboard, exactly as if it were a typewriter. Changes can be made at will, so the writer can experiment with different versions of the manuscript.

Checking. Many word-processing programs include built-in dictionaries containing hundreds of words. With a simple keystroke, the writer can correct every misspelling in the text.

Editing. A few keystrokes can do the work of the old "blue pencil." The writer can add, delete, or move text from one spot to another.

Bluebirds Win
In Alexandria, Virginia, the Bluebirds recorded one of their

Final copy

A newswriter's work may never reach paper until it is printed. Today, most newspapers are produced entirely on computer screens, and many reporters carry portable computers with them on assignment.

Tricks of the trade

Word processors allow writers and editors to do things that were never possible with typewriters.

```
c:
\COMPUTER   1 C:\COMPUTER\CCH3
.........................................
        HELP MENU
F1      delete word
F2      delete line
F3      load new document
F4      print document
F5      indent paragraph
F6      search and replace
F7      save file
F8      alphabetize
F9      run spelling checker
F10     center text on line
```

Word-processing programs can change typefaces, add highlighting, and enlarge or shrink a block of text. Line widths and the spacing of characters can be adjusted to make the text fit the available space. Tables and charts can be created from data stored in compatible spreadsheet programs.

Graphics

Word-processing programs also make it possible to create simple illustrations to accompany text. Some programs include illustrations that are the equivalent of the old paper-and-ink clip art and can be printed in color.

Main cabinet

Floppy disks

Saving text

Text files can be stored on hard or floppy disks. A typical floppy disk can hold about 2,000 pages of text. The files can be printed out on paper whenever a hard copy is required.

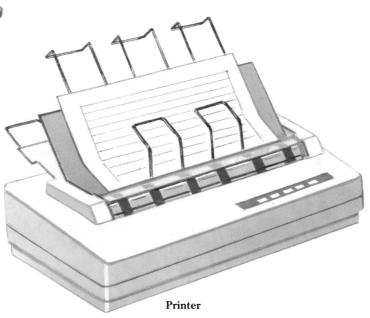

Printer

Can Computers Speak?

Computers equipped with voice synthesizers are capable of mimicking human speech, although the result sometimes sounds flat and unnatural to human ears. The earliest voice synthesizers used a combination of bellows, reeds, and pipes, but now computers that run on electronic circuits produce the sounds. In order to speak, a computer must be told what to say and then be "taught" how to say it according to rules of pronunciation. Each combination of letters produces a predetermined phonetic sound. Voice synthesizers employ two sound sources, one each for vowels and consonants. They produce waveforms that are modified in pitch, volume, stress, and intonation. The waves then pass through a filter that corresponds to a mouth, resulting in a sound that can be understood as a word.

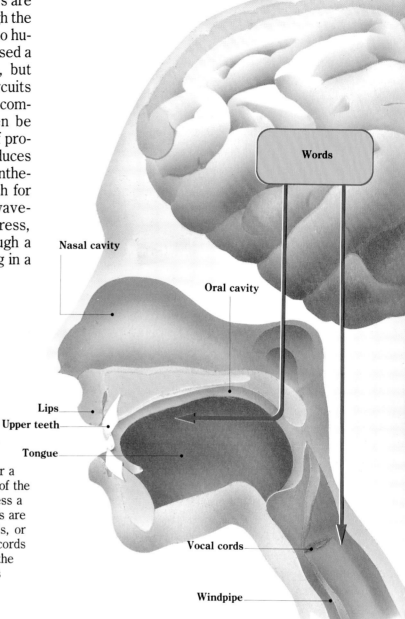

Nasal cavity

Oral cavity

Words

Lips

Upper teeth

Tongue

Vocal cords

Windpipe

The mystery of human speech

Words that begin as thoughts are uttered only after a complex sequence of actions involving many parts of the body takes place. In addition, the brain must process a lot of information to articulate the thoughts. Sounds are produced when air from the lungs passes the glottis, or upper part of the voice box, and causes the vocal cords to vibrate. The sound is modified by the shape of the mouth, the position of the tongue, the way the lips move, and the way breath is used.

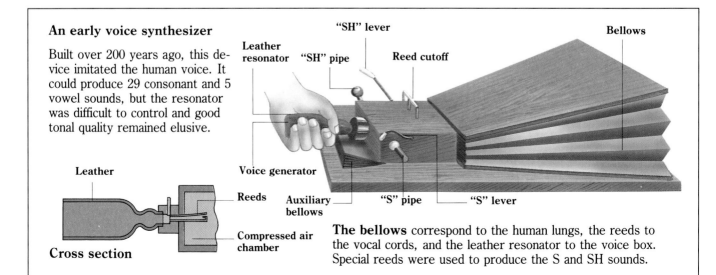

An early voice synthesizer

Built over 200 years ago, this device imitated the human voice. It could produce 29 consonant and 5 vowel sounds, but the resonator was difficult to control and good tonal quality remained elusive.

"SH" lever

Bellows

Leather resonator

"SH" pipe

Reed cutoff

Leather

Voice generator

Reeds

Auxiliary bellows

"S" pipe

"S" lever

Compressed air chamber

Cross section

The bellows correspond to the human lungs, the reeds to the vocal cords, and the leather resonator to the voice box. Special reeds were used to produce the S and SH sounds.

Voice synthesis

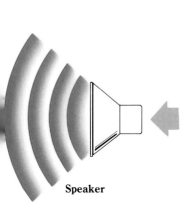

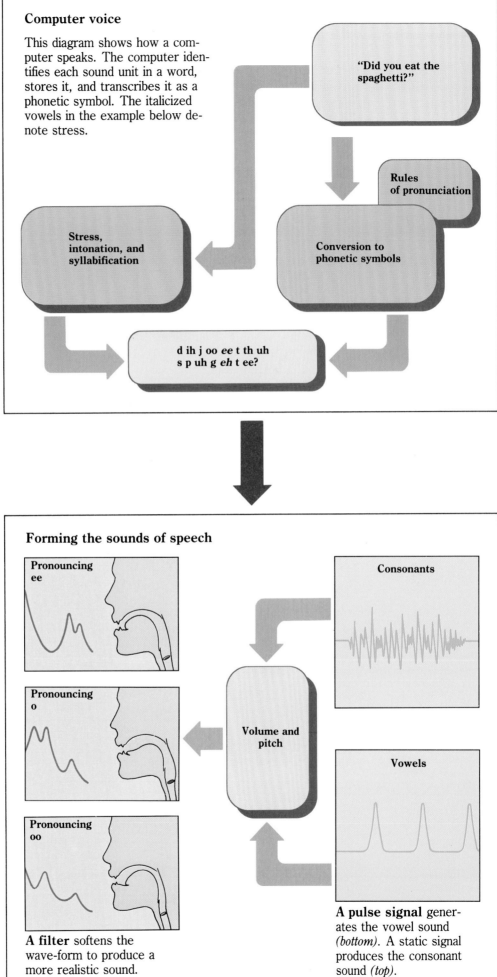

Computer voice

This diagram shows how a computer speaks. The computer identifies each sound unit in a word, stores it, and transcribes it as a phonetic symbol. The italicized vowels in the example below denote stress.

"Did you eat the spaghetti?"

Rules of pronunciation

Conversion to phonetic symbols

Stress, intonation, and syllabification

d ih j oo *ee* t th uh s p uh g *eh* t ee?

Forming the sounds of speech

Pronouncing ee

Pronouncing o

Pronouncing oo

Consonants

Volume and pitch

Vowels

A pulse signal generates the vowel sound *(bottom)*. A static signal produces the consonant sound *(top)*.

A filter softens the wave-form to produce a more realistic sound.

Speaker

61

Can Computers Understand Speech?

When a person hears someone speaking, the inner ears analyze the frequency spectrum of the sound, and the brain understands the words. Some computers can simulate this process with the aid of a spectrum analyzer. Sound signals enter the analyzer through a microphone and are broken down according to their spectral characteristics. The computer then compares these signals with a programmed list of phonemes, or acoustic building blocks. Short time segments of the signal are compared with standard word patterns and rules of language and syntax.

Through this process, a computer can establish what words were spoken. If the program is sophisticated enough, it may even be able to tell from the context whether the spoken word was "through" or "threw." But whether a computer can actually understand speech in the same manner that people do is a hotly debated subject. A computer may be programmed to respond appropriately to particular combinations of words, but does that constitute true understanding? Some experts in the field of artificial intelligence believe that within a few decades, computers will be able to conduct actual, unrestricted conversations with people. Other experts, however, are convinced that computers will always be limited to programmed, rote responses.

Voice recognition

Voice recognition systems consist of three sections: input, analysis, and decision making. The computer makes decisions about the input based on a set of language and syntax rules.

Voice analyzer

Microphone

Spectrum analysis

Sounds produced over several seconds are broken down into very short time segments. The computer then analyzes the frequency of the components of each segment.

Making decisions

From the results of the analysis, the computer decides whether a given word was uttered. The computer compares the stored analysis with a list of possible candidates, then applies rules of syntax and meaning to determine the likelihood that a particular sound corresponds with a particular word.

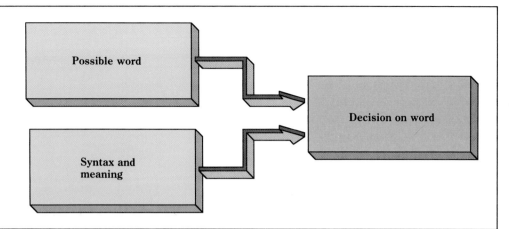

Possible word

Syntax and meaning

Decision on word

Standard speech patterns

The smallest units of speech are expressed in terms of frequency spectra. Standard word patterns tell which units are in a given word.

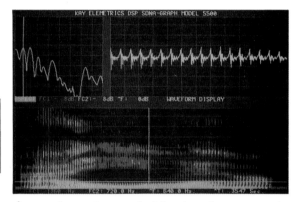

A sound spectrograph *(above)* performs acoustic analysis on the sounds of spoken words. Here, a vowel sound *(upper left)* is compared with a vowel spectrum *(bottom)*.

The human ear

Sound waves cause the eardrum to vibrate. That vibration is then transmitted to several small bones and converted to electrical signals, which are relayed to the brain.

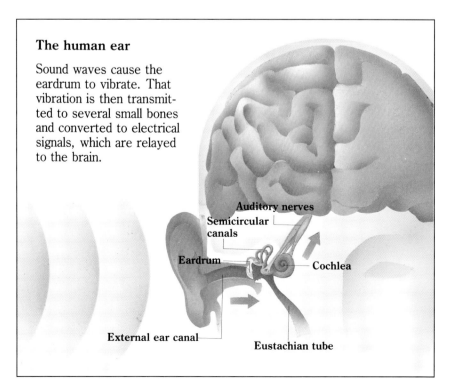

Auditory nerves

Semicircular canals

Eardrum

Cochlea

External ear canal

Eustachian tube

Acoustic analysis

A sound spectrograph displays the spectrum of sound in visible form. In one method of analysis, the normal range of the human voice is broken down into segments, which are color-coded to indicate the strength of the frequency component. Three-dimensional graphs, such as the one above, are another way of visualizing the same information.

Can Computers Read Text?

A human being can glance at the text on this page and instantly recognize the familiar patterns that form letters and words. For a computer to perform the same feat requires special equipment and sophisticated programming. First, an optical scanning device must "read" the text and enter it into the computer. Then the computer must perform an analysis of each character of text to identify the material properly. This task can be complicated by variations in type style and size. The computer must compare each character with stored patterns that identify each letter. Making its best guess about the identity of each character, the computer then stores the complete text for future display or printout. A computer equipped with a voice synthesizer may be capable of reading the text aloud after it has determined the proper syntax, voice stress, and intonation. As computers become more common in everyday life, their ability to take in printed texts and read them aloud will become even more important.

① Scanning input

As the computer scans the pages, it converts the type into electrical signals and stores them into its memory.

scientists refine the algo

to produce the simulation

The image shows 5 of the

million paths that might b

followed by electrons

Reading written text

Text identified by character recognition is analyzed structurally. This process uses a dictionary and syntax stored in the computer's memory. Artificial intelligence determines where the breaks between syllables occur. Additional software supplies information on pronunciation, stress, and intonation, and a voice synthesizer reads the text aloud.

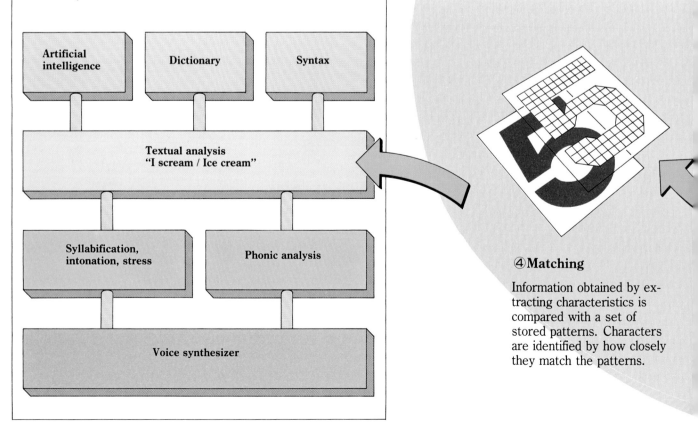

| Artificial intelligence | Dictionary | Syntax |

Textual analysis
"I scream / Ice cream"

| Syllabification, intonation, stress | Phonic analysis |

Voice synthesizer

④ Matching

Information obtained by extracting characteristics is compared with a set of stored patterns. Characters are identified by how closely they match the patterns.

■ Character recognition

Computers identify characters, graphics, and sounds through the process of pattern recognition. While sounds are analyzed by frequency distribution, printed material is identified by comparing characters step by step with a set of stored shapes and patterns.

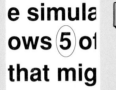

② Preprocessing

The character patterns are converted to binary numbers: 1s for the dark portions and 0s for the light portions.

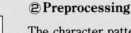

③ Extraction

The computer extracts the identifying elements of each character from the binary pattern by one of several methods.

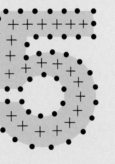

- Edge pixels
- + Core line

◀ **Thinning.** Scanners remove pixels from the edge of the image and apply pattern analysis to the center, or core line. Loops are analyzed by eight directional vectors.

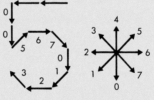

+ Contour points
⊕ Contact points

Text scanner

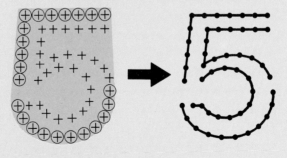

Shape analysis. Polygonal figures *(above, pink)* survey the shape of the character. The character is analyzed according to where it makes contact with the polygons.

▲ **Background analysis.** As the computer scans in four directions, labels are affixed to each portion of the character, indicating whether or not there is a pixel in that location.

How Do Computers Make Music?

Computers first made music in the 1950s when composers Lejaren Hiller and Leonard Isaacson wrote the *Illiac Suite for String Quartet* with the aid of a computer. But the suite, named after the computer, was played by a human string quartet. Today, computers can not only compose, but also can play music in a wide range of styles. A computer can compose after it solves a predetermined algorithm designed to yield a succession of musical notes. Sounds can be produced by synthesizing wave-forms according to calculations or by using a computer to control an oscillator.

By the 1970s, computerized music synthesizers had become as common as guitars at rock concerts. But creative musicians have also experimented with ways of introducing computers to the world of classical music in both composition and performance. The highly mathematical nature of music makes it a wide-open field of artistic endeavor for computers.

Synthesizing music

Frequency modulation can produce a rich tone using only a few oscillators and is the most common form of music synthesis. A carrier wave *(right)* is modulated by another wave *(center right)* resulting in a synthesized wave-form *(far right)* that is fed through the oscillators to produce the actual sound.

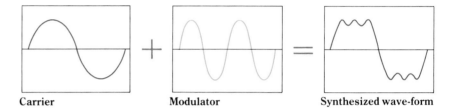

Carrier   Modulator   Synthesized wave-form

Composition and performance

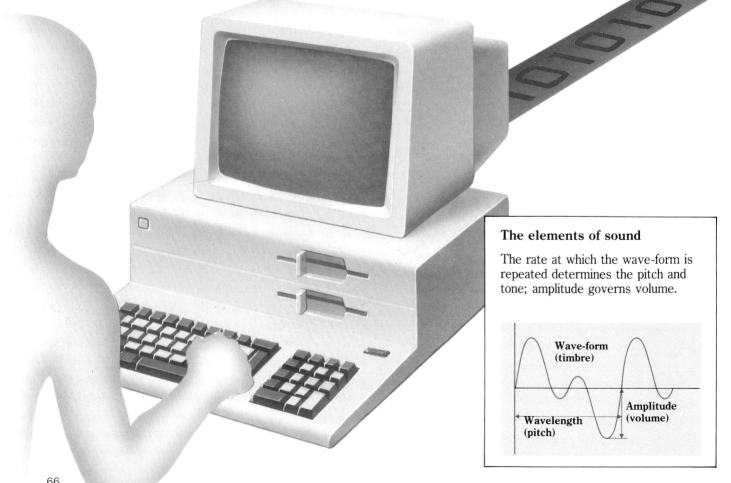

The elements of sound

The rate at which the wave-form is repeated determines the pitch and tone; amplitude governs volume.

Wave-form (timbre)

Amplitude (volume)

Wavelength (pitch)

The structure of sound. Since all sounds are composed of sound waves, it is possible to devise a mathematical description of any sound, such as that of a violin. Computers calculate the numerical values of particular sounds and convert the values to voltages, which are passed through amplifiers to a speaker. Computers may also feed specified parameters to oscillators. This way a computer may reproduce the sound of a performance by human musicians, or it may even create entirely new sounds, depending on the parameters of the algorithm.

An amplifier increases the amplitude of the electrical wave-form and sends it to a speaker, where it is converted into vibrations in the air.

A balancing filter softens the individual steps obtained from the digital/analog converter into a smooth, continuously changing wave-form.

A digital/analog converter cuts the sound wave into short time segments and expresses the amplitude—or changes in air-pressure intensity—and frequency at these points in numerical values, which, in turn, control the voltages in the amplifier.

A digital synthesizer turns numbers into music. Since any waveform can be described numerically, virtually any sound can be created by a synthesizer that is controlled by a computer.

Computer composition

The *Illiac Suite for String Quartet* was composed by calculating numerical chains using a transition probability, which established the probability of moving from one given note to another. This probability may be determined from random numbers, from statistical analysis of existing works, or from a table, such as the one below, stating the probability of moving from the last note, F, of the score to the next one.

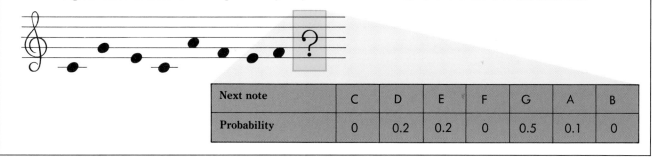

Next note	C	D	E	F	G	A	B
Probability	0	0.2	0.2	0	0.5	0.1	0

How Do Humans and Computers Differ?

The British nineteenth-century mathematician William Shanks spent most of his life calculating the value of pi to the 707th decimal place. A computer can perform the same calculation in less than a second. For speed and accuracy of calculation, computers are vastly superior to human beings. Computers also can quickly store and retrieve vast amounts of information that would overwhelm a human's memory. Yet computers are limited in their ability to analyze and understand information, while humans can recognize patterns and discriminate between relevant and irrelevant information. Humans are especially good at learning from experience. A computer analyzing a map to find the best route from point A to point B would sort through every possible combination of routes, regardless of their relative practicality. A human, relying on relevant experiences, such as rush-hour traffic jams and dangerous intersections, could quickly find the best route. Computers lack the human ability to size up a situation and judge from experience. They also lack that most important and elusive human quality: imagination.

Different ways of thinking

How computers think

A computer performs rapid calculations of data according to the instructions in its program. For some problems, such as the puzzle of doors and mazes at left, computers can quickly sort through all possible solutions and find the best one much more quickly than a human could.

How humans think

A human's thought processes are more flexible than a computer's. All of a person's knowledge can be mobilized to solve a single problem. Below, an arrow represents thought. The arrow's path will vary from person to person.

Artificial intelligence (AI)

Artificial intelligence is a field of study aimed at providing computers with characteristics of human thought, such as the ability to infer solutions to problems based on past experience. In computers equipped with artificial intelligence capabilities, learned information becomes knowledge.

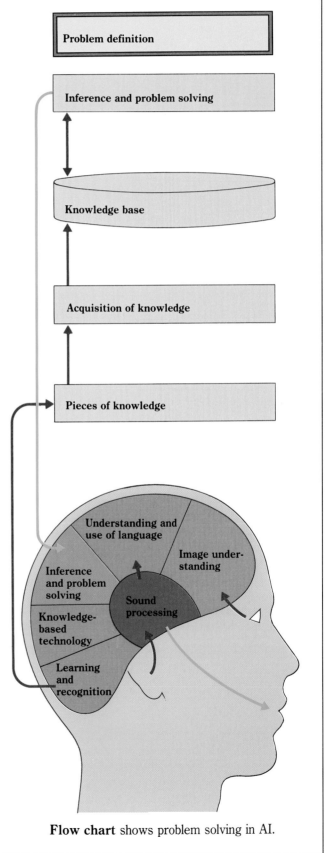

Flow chart shows problem solving in AI.

4

Computer Graphics

The first computers generated simplistic and unrealistic images. But today, computers can produce images that are virtually indistinguishable from photographs. Many of the most stunning special effects in motion pictures are generated by computers. Even a personal computer (PC) can create complex graphics. Many PC screens can display 256,000 picture elements, or pixels, with 640 pixels arranged horizontally and 400 vertically. If each pixel has eight bits, then a pixel can display eight colors, and in combination they can make an on-screen palette of 256 different hues. Since the processing speed of computers has increased, PCs can also display animated computer images.

New levels of detail have been achieved thanks to the use of fractals, a branch of mathematics that deals with shapes. Computers used to be limited to forming regular, geometric shapes, but fractals have made it possible to create mathematical descriptions of irregular, natural shapes such as leaves, clouds, and coastlines. These new graphics capabilities have applications for the world of art as well as for science and technology. Artists have used computers to create aesthetically pleasing images of the real world and to depict extravagant and breathtaking scenes that previously existed only in the imagination.

In a computer's tribute to life, the image at right shows a model symbolizing natural growth and propagation, rendered with an artistic flair by Japanese computer artist Yoichiro Kawaguchi.

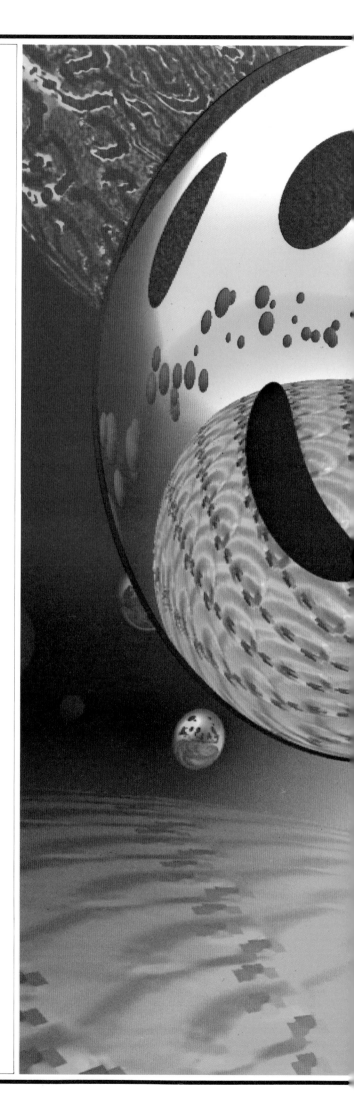

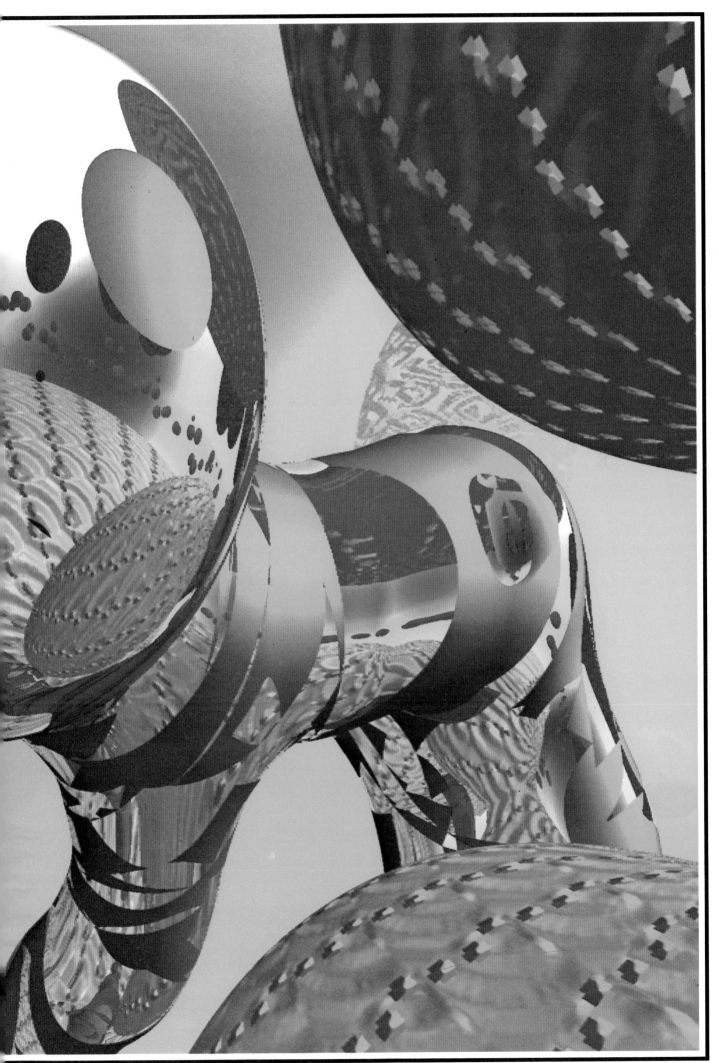

How Does a Computer Create an Image of a Human Face?

Computers can create images of complex three-dimensional objects, such as a human face, by using two different methods. In one method, the computer begins with a regular solid shape—a sphere or an ellipsoid, for example—and makes modifications as instructed. A more exact method consists of entering the details of a three-dimensional map of the subject and instructing the computer to reproduce those details. Color

photographs together with grids that were projected on the subject's face provide data for a structural model. Then the operator adds surface elements to give the computer image a realistic texture. Additional color and shading provide a lifelike quality. Because the computer's memory holds information about the face in three dimensions, the monitor is able to show the image from many different angles.

Creating the image

The diagram at right shows the information needed and the sequential steps by which a computer can reproduce an image.

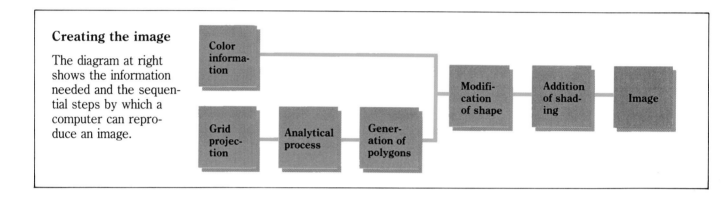

Color information

Grid projection

Analytical process

Generation of polygons

Modification of shape

Addition of shading

Image

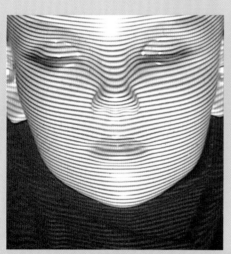

▲ **Grid projection** on subject's face

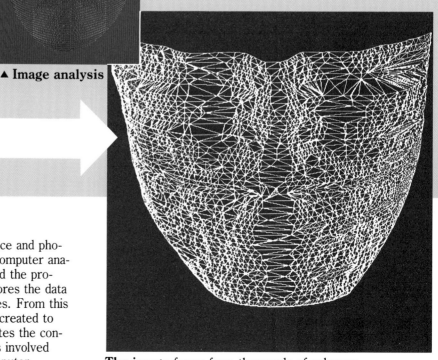

▲ **Image analysis**

The image forms from thousands of polygons.

From grid to polygons

A grid of parallel lines is projected onto a face and photographed with an electronic camera. The computer analyzes the difference between the original and the projected grids to obtain structural data and stores the data in the form of a table, listing grid coordinates. From this data, polygonal, or many-sided, shapes are created to form a three-dimensional image that duplicates the contours of the actual face. The many polygons involved make this process impossible without a computer.

Rotation

Once it has data on three dimensions, the computer can rotate the image and show what the face would look like viewed from different angles.

Frontal view

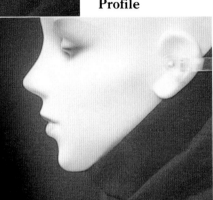

Profile

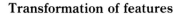

Transformation of features

Computers lend valuable assistance in surgery. By manipulating facial features on the computer, a doctor can show a person's appearance before and after plastic surgery.

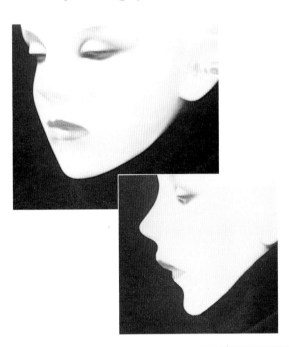

From photo to screen

▲ **Color photograph of subject**

Final display of computer-generated image

Adding color and shading

The operator instructs the computer to add color to the polygons to match the data from the photograph. Red, blue, and green are processed in 256 subtle gradations to provide realistic tones. A light source can be added at any location, creating shadows that heighten the realism of the image. Data from these calculations is then written to the screen memory and sent to the CRT display. The final image is virtually identical to a photograph.

How Are Computers Used to Help Design Automobiles?

Computer-aided design and computer-aided manufacturing, known as CAD/CAM, have revolutionized the process of designing automobiles, aircraft, and other vehicles. Formerly, car designers modeled a prototype in clay, then carefully measured the model to make the stamping dies. By creating a model on a computer, designers now achieve greater precision in both design and manufacture than ever before. Rather than placing clay models in wind tunnels to test a car's aerodynamic characteristics, designers can subject computer models to tests to assure the stability and good performance of the design. Similarly, a car's strength can be tested without the expense of actually crashing an automobile. Computers also test such factors as vibration, heat conduction, and visibility. Even the car's interior can be modeled in the computer to achieve the most efficient design of the engine, dashboard, and passenger compartment.

Body design

Computers play a major role in the design of automobiles. The graphics give designers more versatility and can produce greater detail than the clay models of old.

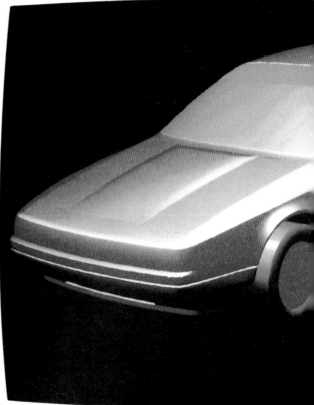

Computerized automotive design

A CAD terminal for automotive design

A simulated collision

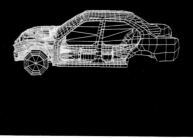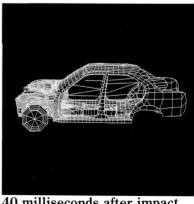

Before impact   **20 milliseconds after impact**   **40 milliseconds after impact**

Visibility simulation

The computer can calculate and display the field of vision from the driver's seat.

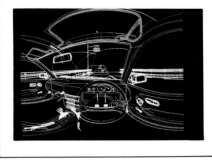

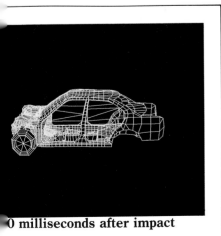

0 milliseconds after impact

Aerodynamics

A car's stability, road-holding performance, and fuel economy are all affected by the way air flows over its body when it is in motion. Lines representing airflow, below and right, show areas of high and low pressure. Supercomputers must be used to analyze the complex eddies created by the airflow.

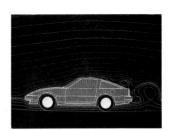

Components and parts

Once designers decide on the external styling, they must find room for the internal parts and components. Two-dimensional drawings make this a difficult task, but a computer can test different arrangements, move components, and study the interrelationships in three dimensions.

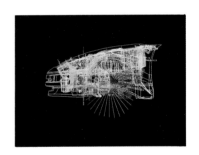

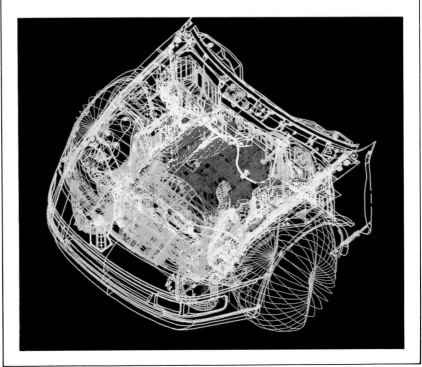

How Do Computers Make Maps?

Computers completely changed cartography because they simplified the assembly and display of all the complex data that goes into the making of a map. Information on geomorphology—that is, the basic shape of the land—from aerial and satellite surveys can be digitized and stored in a computer for use in a variety of maps. Similarly, existing maps can be scanned and digitized for use by a computer, then easily updated. The map database may also include information on cities, roads, railways, vegetation, relief, and land use.

Because all of this information is stored digitally in the computer, it can be rearranged in different ways to create maps for many purposes. For example, a map of a city's water and sewer pipes can be used to analyze the network and develop measures to stop leakage. Such a map can also be expanded to include gas pipes, electric power lines, and anything else that is installed underground. When a city installs new systems, the computer map can be updated quickly, without the necessity of drawing a completely new map.

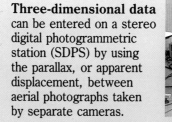

Three-dimensional data can be entered on a stereo digital photogrammetric station (SDPS) by using the parallax, or apparent displacement, between aerial photographs taken by separate cameras.

Data is digitized by moving a mouse over a map or structural drawing and entering coordinates for each feature.

Computer mapping

Map data from different sources can be digitized and stored in the computer memory. The data can then be processed to create special-purpose maps.

Work station for a map information system

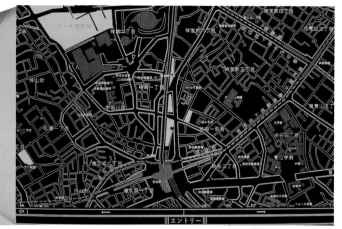

Urban planning can be facilitated by a map designed to highlight information about houses and buildings, as in this map of a city in Japan.

● Map information database

Database layers

Road layer

Building layer

Pipe layer

Different types of map information can be recorded together in separate layers of a computer database. The information can be retrieved separately or combined as needed.

Construction plans may rely on maps that have information on pipes and other buried systems and that highlight the data so builders will know where not to dig.

From maps to graphics

The same database that is used to make maps may also be used to create computer graphics of the area being mapped. This capability demonstrates the versatility of computer mapping. The graphic display at right shows Japan's Mount Fuji.

How Do Computer Games Work?

On-screen characters

The child's image is made up of 24 characters in the program's character map.

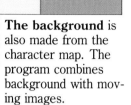

The background is also made from the character map. The program combines background with moving images.

Program

Data for screen use

● **TV game player**

The game unit contains a microprocessor chip and has a slot into which the game cartridge is inserted. Data and programs are stored in the cartridge, and additional instructions are entered by the players using the controllers.

● **Game flow**

Game cartridge

The game program and data stored in the cartridge are read into the computer.

In the early days of computing, operators sometimes invented games to play on their computers in their spare time. What began as idle amusement has become a billion-dollar industry. Today, many of the most popular computer games do not require a personal computer; players use a special-purpose computer in a box hooked to their television set instead. The games' software cartridges contain a program and screen instructions that are processed, then sent to the TV. A controller—a joystick or a mouse—converts a player's movements into digital signals that are transmitted to the program. The program interprets these signals and creates screen displays to match the movements. Screen data is processed in groups of several pixels, rather than by individual ones, to save bits and increase speed. These groups are called characters, created on an internal map, and include both moving images and stationary background images.

Generating a picture

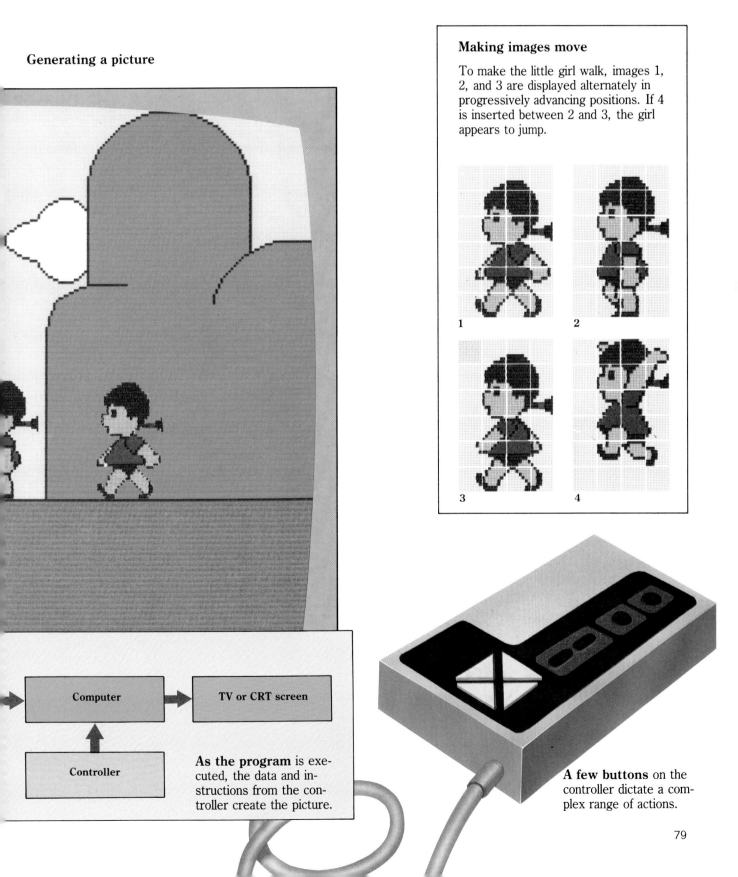

Making images move

To make the little girl walk, images 1, 2, and 3 are displayed alternately in progressively advancing positions. If 4 is inserted between 2 and 3, the girl appears to jump.

1

2

3

4

Computer

TV or CRT screen

Controller

As the program is executed, the data and instructions from the controller create the picture.

A few buttons on the controller dictate a complex range of actions.

How Are Special Effects Created?

"How did they do that?" people often wonder when they see a stunning special effects sequence in a movie or television program. Increasingly, directors do it with computers. For example, a spaceship zooms past a planet, while the ship's captain is seen through a viewport. To create such a scene, a computer-controlled camera moves past a stationary model of the spaceship; on film, it is the ship that seems to move. Using a process called chroma key, the crew films the background as if the cameras were on the ship and combines that footage with the film of the ship. The actors are photographed separately, and that film is inserted into a window in the sequence. Computers can combine many different pieces of film into a single scene.

In the video editing room, operators view the images on several different screens. Computers are used to coordinate the images and combine them into a single scene. The chroma key process uses color variation as the key to positioning different images.

The magic of chroma key

Foreground image

Blank out foreground image; replace with white silhouette from below.

Conversion: blue to white, all other colors to black

Background blacked out

Black/white reversal

Image reversed

Subject silhouetted

Background image

Blank out white image signal.

Background with foreground

80

The combined foreground and background images create a new scene.

 Matrix. Generate a monochrome signal from a reference color—red, green, or blue—usually blue.

● Key. Blank out white image signal.

▼ Synthesize. Combine the images.

⬡ Reverse black and white signals.

Chroma key uses three primary color signals—red, green, and blue—from the video camera. The differences in the signals are the key for extracting images. If an object is photographed against a blue background and the monochrome image is keyed to the blue signal, the background appears white and the object black. This is then reversed, and the extracted images are combined—bringing the Statue of Liberty to Niagara Falls.

Synthesized images

A ship in port can appear to be sailing through the Suez Canal or along the coast of Japan. First, the ship is photographed against a blue-screen background. Later, the chroma key technique will be used to combine footage of the ship with film from the desired background location.

The ship is filmed on the blue-screen background.

A blue screen is set up at left.

From on board ship, any background can be viewed.

How Does a Flight Simulator Work?

A flight simulator allows pilot trainees to learn their craft without ever leaving the ground. To familiarize the pilot with his working environment, the cockpit of an actual plane is duplicated down to the last rivet. This cockpit is mounted on hydraulic pumps that can tilt the room to match the simulated movements of the aircraft. A CRT display replaces the windshield, giving the pilot a view of a graphic representation of actual scenes encountered during flight, takeoff, and landing. A computer controls the images as well as the readings on the cockpit instrument displays. Everything affecting the flight is stored in the computer, from weather conditions, local topography, and runway dimensions, to the brightness and angle of the sun and shadows. The speed, direction of movement, and attitude of the aircraft are also factored into the computer's calculations. To reduce the computational burden on the computer, the hardware includes a series of processors in pipeline formation that operate in parallel, each generating a different segment of the view displayed in the window. For the same reason, the images seen through the windshield are simplified. The goal of the simulation is to duplicate precisely the conditions of an actual flight, so that a pilot can gain experience without the expense and possible danger of flying a real plane. Difficult conditions, such as landing during a storm, can be simulated and repeated as often as necessary. Flight simulators are used in civilian and military aviation throughout the world.

A simulated landing

Miles of terrain appear on the computer screen as a trainee goes through the motions of landing an airplane. Illustrations 1 through 4 show how an airplane approaches, descends, lands, and taxis along the runway. Any airport can be used in a simulation.

1

2

3

A flight simulator system

Different computers handle various simulations, such as instrument displays, field of view display, and hydraulic movement. Each computer works in conjunction with the others to produce a realistic scenario.

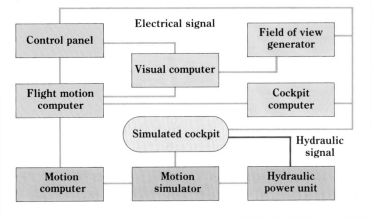

Electrical signal

Control panel

Field of view generator

Visual computer

Flight motion computer

Cockpit computer

Simulated cockpit

Hydraulic signal

Motion computer

Motion simulator

Hydraulic power unit

4

Pilot's seat

Copilot's seat

On-board control panel

On-board testing officer's seat

Flight simulator

Hydraulic legs expand or contract beneath a computer-operated cockpit. The computer calculates the exact motions of the aircraft in response to information from the controls, then drives the hydraulic unit to create the proper motions.

Hydraulic cylinder

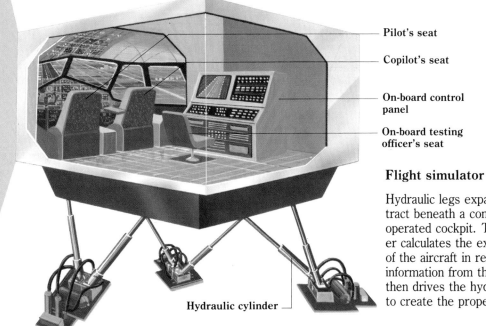

5
Digitizing Daily Life

As scientists and engineers struggled to develop the electronic digital computer in the 1940s, few people glimpsed the potential of the new machine. The first computers were balky contraptions, difficult to program and likely to break down. Their exorbitant cost placed them beyond the reach of most users except for large corporations and governments. Computers, it seemed, would never enjoy widespread use.

Over the next few decades, however, three developments enabled the computer to transform modern society. First, computers got smaller. The tasks done by room-size computers of the 1940s can now be handled by desktop machines. Second, computers grew more powerful. Modern supercomputers are at least one million times faster than their sluggish ancestors; they are also easier to program and far more versatile. And third, computers became cheaper. A personal computer now has greater computing capability than the multimillion-dollar machines from the dawn of the computer age.

Together these changes have helped computers pervade all aspects of everyday life, from writing a report to watching a video to checking one's wrist watch for the time. At home, at school, or at work, it is virtually impossible to go through a day without using a computer. Meanwhile, engineers are working to make the machines smaller, more powerful, and less expensive. It seems certain that the computer's impact on society will continue to grow.

First developed for military, business, and academic use, computers have begun to reshape activities in the home as well.

What Are Bar Codes?

A bar code—the familiar sequence of black and white lines that appears on products sold in stores—is a binary code similar to that used by computers. The sequence of the alternating black and white bars enable manufacturers and retailers to encode and monitor a great deal of information about a product: its identity, its price, and its place of origin.

When a consumer buys an item in a store, a clerk passes the item over a scanner—a machine that shines a beam of light across the code. The light bounces off the code and back into the scanner, where it hits a light-sensitive device called a photodetector. Because the white lines reflect the beam more strongly than the black lines, the photodetector can turn the reflected light into an electronic binary signal; the scanner then sends this signal to the cash register and to the store's computer. The result is faster sales transactions and automatic tracking of inventory.

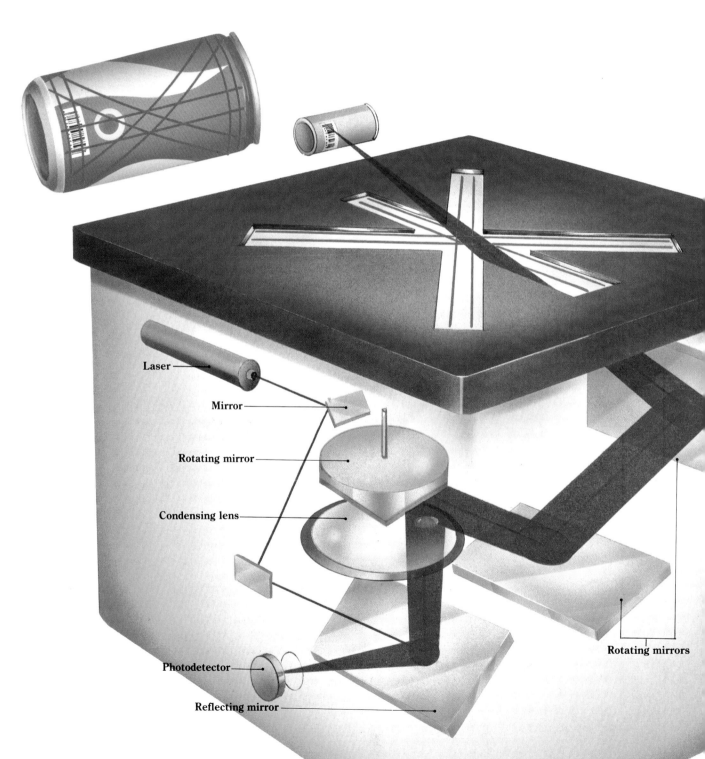

Laser

Mirror

Rotating mirror

Condensing lens

Photodetector

Reflecting mirror

Rotating mirrors

Taking stock of supplies

With every sale, the scanner sends the information contained in the product's bar code to the store's computer. The computer subtracts the item from its inventory and informs the central computer of the transaction. Based on the frequency of sales, the central computer reorders products as needed.

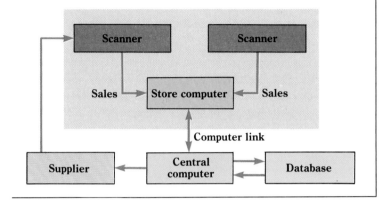

A bar code's secret language

Each bar code has room for 113 lines. A black line corresponds to a binary 1, a white line to a 0. Every group of seven lines represents a number, which appears below the code. In this example, 0110011 stands for the number 9 and indicates the product's country of origin.

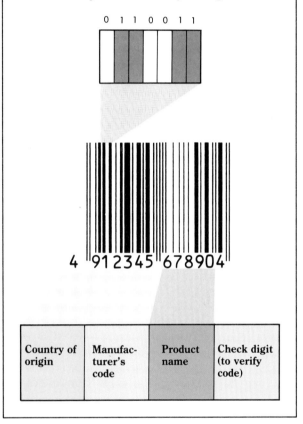

Country of origin	Manufacturer's code	Product name	Check digit (to verify code)

A scanner at work

The fixed type of scanner, shown at left, is most commonly used in supermarkets. Housed inside a checkout counter, the fixed scanner shoots a beam of laser light up through a window in the counter's surface. Rotating mirrors direct the beam along crisscrossing paths until it hits the bar code. The light that is reflected from the bar code passes back through the window and is channeled by mirrors to the photodetector.

Hand-held scanners

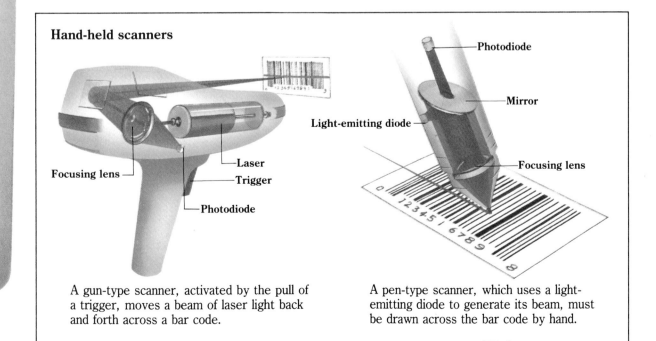

A gun-type scanner, activated by the pull of a trigger, moves a beam of laser light back and forth across a bar code.

A pen-type scanner, which uses a light-emitting diode to generate its beam, must be drawn across the bar code by hand.

How Do Bank Machines Work?

An automated-teller machine (ATM) performs simple banking functions such as deposits, withdrawals, and transfers between accounts. Introduced in the late 1960s, ATMs caught on by virtue of their convenience: Not only do they operate 24 hours a day, but their small size allows them to be installed virtually anywhere.

When someone opens a bank account, the bank usually issues that person an ATM access card. On the back of the card is a magnetic strip containing a coded number assigned exclusively to that card. To use an ATM, a patron inserts the access card into the machine and enters his or her personal identification number, or PIN. Then, using the machine's keypad, the customer instructs the ATM what to do. When the transaction is complete, the ATM returns the access card and issues a printed record.

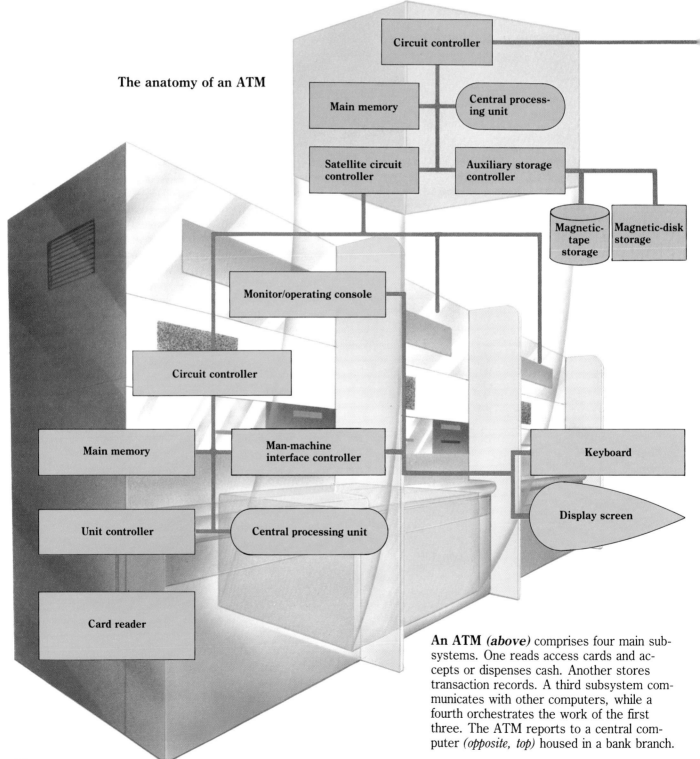

The anatomy of an ATM

An ATM *(above)* comprises four main subsystems. One reads access cards and accepts or dispenses cash. Another stores transaction records. A third subsystem communicates with other computers, while a fourth orchestrates the work of the first three. The ATM reports to a central computer *(opposite, top)* housed in a bank branch.

A financial mastermind

A bank's central computer may control dozens of automated-teller machines. When an ATM transaction is relayed to this computer, the computer calculates a new balance for the customer's account. It also keeps a master list of transactions.

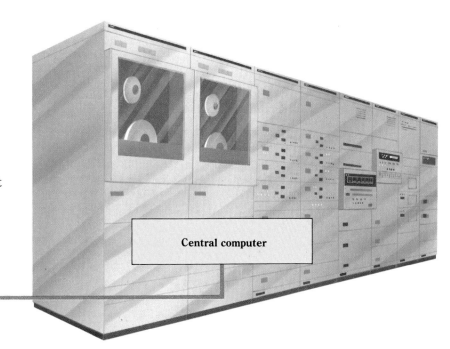

Central computer

Magnetic card

The route from card to cash

Before allowing a transaction, an ATM verifies the patron's PIN. For security, the PIN is not kept in the computer; instead, the ATM checks an offset number, a code that determines if the PIN is valid.

Many people now visit an automated-teller machine, rather than a bank branch, to carry out simple financial transactions.

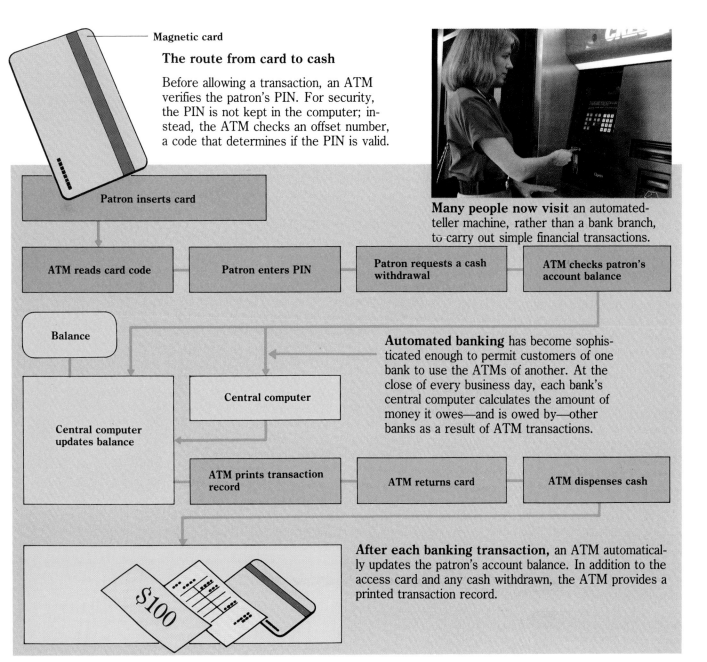

Patron inserts card

ATM reads card code

Patron enters PIN

Patron requests a cash withdrawal

ATM checks patron's account balance

Balance

Central computer

Central computer updates balance

ATM prints transaction record

ATM returns card

ATM dispenses cash

$100

Automated banking has become sophisticated enough to permit customers of one bank to use the ATMs of another. At the close of every business day, each bank's central computer calculates the amount of money it owes—and is owed by—other banks as a result of ATM transactions.

After each banking transaction, an ATM automatically updates the patron's account balance. In addition to the access card and any cash withdrawn, the ATM provides a printed transaction record.

What Is a Pocket Computer?

As its name implies, a pocket computer is small enough to fit in the user's pocket. It is roughly the size of a calculator, but far more versatile; offering alphabetic as well as numeric keys, a pocket computer is capable of complex programming and word processing in addition to standard calculations. A pocket computer also boasts a larger screen than a calculator and is often able to display graphics. Certain models can even be linked to a larger computer, thereby putting the power of a mainframe into the user's pocket.

Because they are so small, pocket computers allow people to turn any locale—a hotel room, an airport lounge, a restaurant table—into an office. Such portability has made the devices especially popular among people whose work requires a great deal of travel. By the early 1990s, in fact, demand for the machines had turned pocket computers into the fastest-growing sector of the computer industry.

Features of a pocket computer

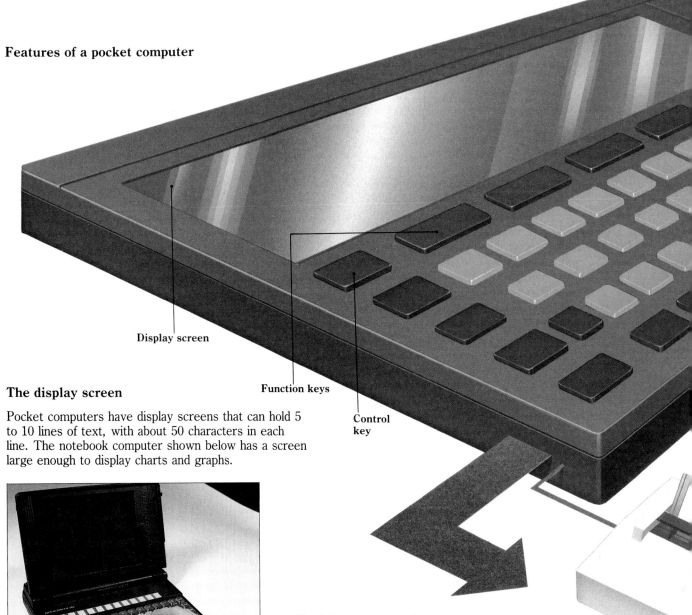

Display screen

Function keys

Control key

The display screen

Pocket computers have display screens that can hold 5 to 10 lines of text, with about 50 characters in each line. The notebook computer shown below has a screen large enough to display charts and graphs.

Hooking up to a printer

By plugging the pocket computer into a compatible printer, the user can print out any file stored in the machine's memory.

When additional memory space is needed to run complex programs, more memory cards like the two shown here can be added.

From one computer to another

Through the use of a modem, which transmits data over telephone lines, a pocket computer can exchange information with other computers.

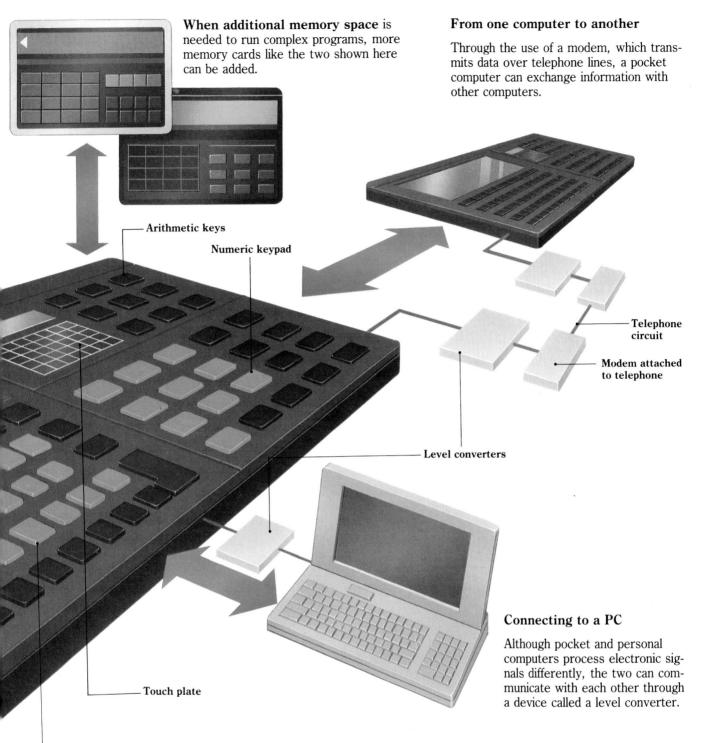

Arithmetic keys

Numeric keypad

Telephone circuit

Modem attached to telephone

Level converters

Touch plate

Alphabetic keys

Connecting to a PC

Although pocket and personal computers process electronic signals differently, the two can communicate with each other through a device called a level converter.

An electronic diary

A pocket computer often serves as an electronic calendar—a high-capacity catchall for schedules, addresses, phone numbers, and notes. Because of its specific function, a pocket calendar usually has fewer keys than a general-purpose pocket computer. A special ROM card can turn the calendar into a dictionary, a spellchecker, a thesaurus, or a language translator.

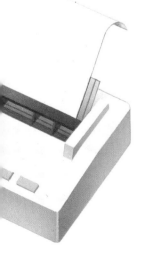

Why Does a Business Use Computers?

Computers have become essential for businesses of every size. In addition to their standard roles—chiefly word processing and number crunching—business computers can help managers make more intelligent and economical decisions. Able to arrange and analyze information at the stroke of a key, a business computer can be used to issue economic forecasts, plan a company's growth, or avoid waste.

As shown in the illustration below, a typical business has a central computer—a mainframe for larger firms, a so-called minicomputer for smaller ones—that supports a word processor or a personal computer at each employee's work station. When the work stations are interconnected through a data network, colleagues are able to exchange information and ideas almost instantaneously.

Toward the paperless office

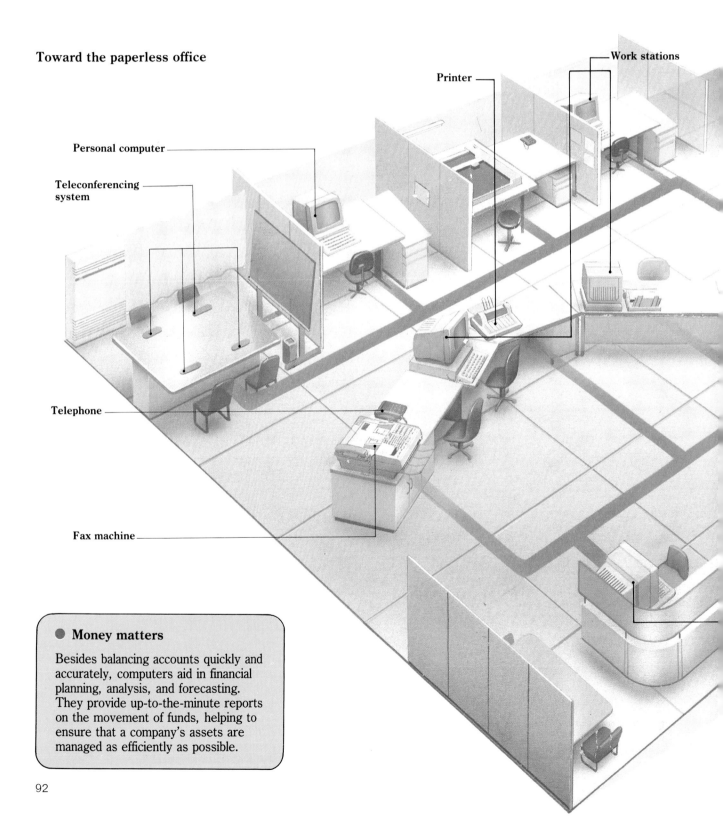

Personal computer

Teleconferencing system

Telephone

Fax machine

Printer

Work stations

● **Money matters**

Besides balancing accounts quickly and accurately, computers aid in financial planning, analysis, and forecasting. They provide up-to-the-minute reports on the movement of funds, helping to ensure that a company's assets are managed as efficiently as possible.

Digital divisions

Most companies contain a number of divisions. A manufacturing company, for example, has separate departments for management, personnel, marketing, and production. A firm's use of computers is intended to simplify the work of each division and help them communicate with one another.

● Management

Without computers, the sheer volume of information monitored by a company might overwhelm the firm's ability to track it. Computers keep tabs on every aspect of a business, no matter how detailed, and give managers instant access to that information.

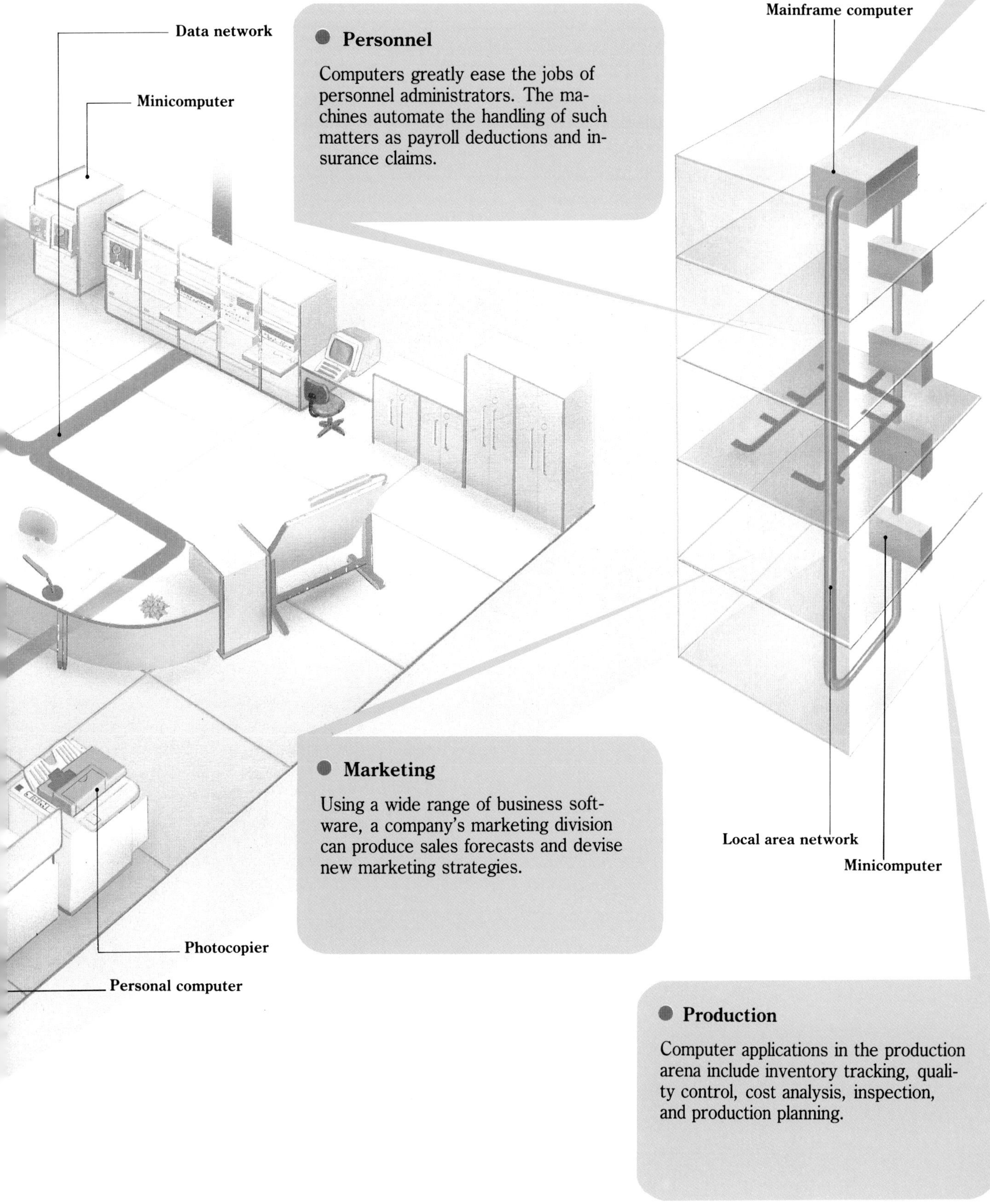

Data network

Minicomputer

Mainframe computer

● Personnel

Computers greatly ease the jobs of personnel administrators. The machines automate the handling of such matters as payroll deductions and insurance claims.

● Marketing

Using a wide range of business software, a company's marketing division can produce sales forecasts and devise new marketing strategies.

Local area network

Minicomputer

Photocopier

Personal computer

● Production

Computer applications in the production arena include inventory tracking, quality control, cost analysis, inspection, and production planning.

What Is Electronic Publishing?

Electronic publishing is the process whereby computers perform all the tasks necessary to produce a publication. Without computers, the different parts of a publication—text, illustrations, and graphics—must be created individually, then cut out and pasted down to form a layout. Each layout—one per page in a newspaper, one per spread, or two facing pages, in a magazine or book—serves as the template for making printing plates. These plates are used to print the final product. For publishers who still work this way, it is a tedious and time-consuming process.

Computers eliminate many of these mechanical steps. A device called a scanner lets an editor digitize pictures—that is, transform them into digital signals that can be processed by a computer. As shown below, the editor then arranges the elements of the publication on a display screen. Additional computer technology, in the form of a printer that uses lasers to produce extremely sharp, clear type, provides professional-looking hard copy—so called because it exists on paper rather than in electronic, or soft, form.

The development of computer equipment for publishing has spawned a new industry, desktop publishing, in which individuals compose and distribute high-caliber documents from their offices or homes. Publishing—once the preserve of large companies—has become a very real option for anyone with access to a computer.

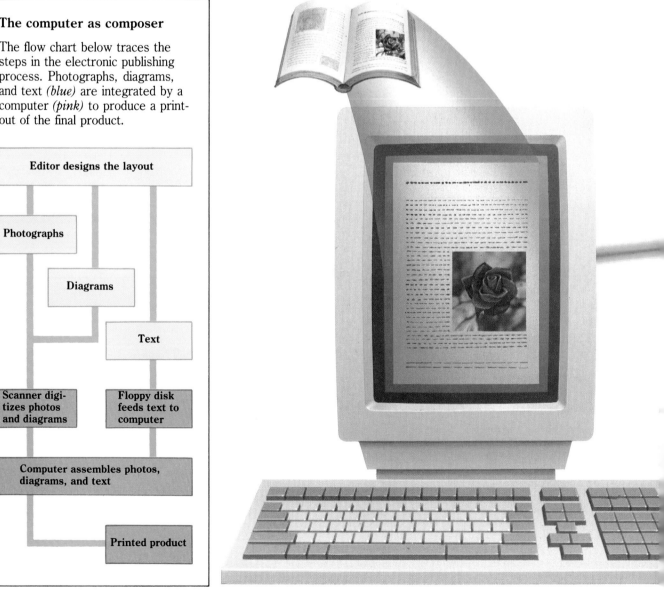

The computer as composer

The flow chart below traces the steps in the electronic publishing process. Photographs, diagrams, and text *(blue)* are integrated by a computer *(pink)* to produce a print-out of the final product.

Editor designs the layout

Photographs

Diagrams

Text

Scanner digitizes photos and diagrams

Floppy disk feeds text to computer

Computer assembles photos, diagrams, and text

Printed product

A digital Gutenberg

Electronic publishing features a series of auto-mated steps. First, a scanner digitizes any illustrations. Next, the editor changes the text as necessary. Third, the editor creates a space in the layout for the picture, wrapping the text around the space. Finally, the editor instructs the computer to insert the photo into the space. The layout is now ready to be printed.

Editing terminal

Local area network

A scanner: color by numbers

Every color in a printed illustration can be represented by a mix of red, yellow, blue, and black. A scanner divides a picture into tiny sections called pixels (for "picture elements") and assigns each pixel four numbers indicating the intensity of its four constituent colors. The scanner then sends these numbers to the computer, which translates them into an image on the screen.

Laser printer

Computer

The warehouse called CD-ROM

Using a storage device known as CD-ROM (compact disk-read-only memory), a computer can call up pages of a publication that have been digitized on a compact disk—much like the CDs that play music—and display them on a video screen. One CD-ROM disk can store an entire encyclopedia.

How Do Airline Computers Work?

To allocate airplane seats to passengers in the most efficient way possible, almost all major airlines rely on a computerized reservation system, or CRS. A typical CRS comprises a database containing information about every seat on every flight scheduled by the airline, plus a computer to process the requests for those seats. Airline employees and travel agents use their computer terminals to gain access to the CRS and to reserve seats on a specific flight.

The reservation process is ideally suited to computerization. The existence of a central database allows travelers from all over the world to find out in seconds whether a seat is available on a flight to the destination of their choice. If a seat happens to be available on more than one flight, the traveler can pick the flight with the lowest fare. A CRS also benefits the airlines; it enables a carrier to book each flight as close to capacity as possible, thus maximizing profits.

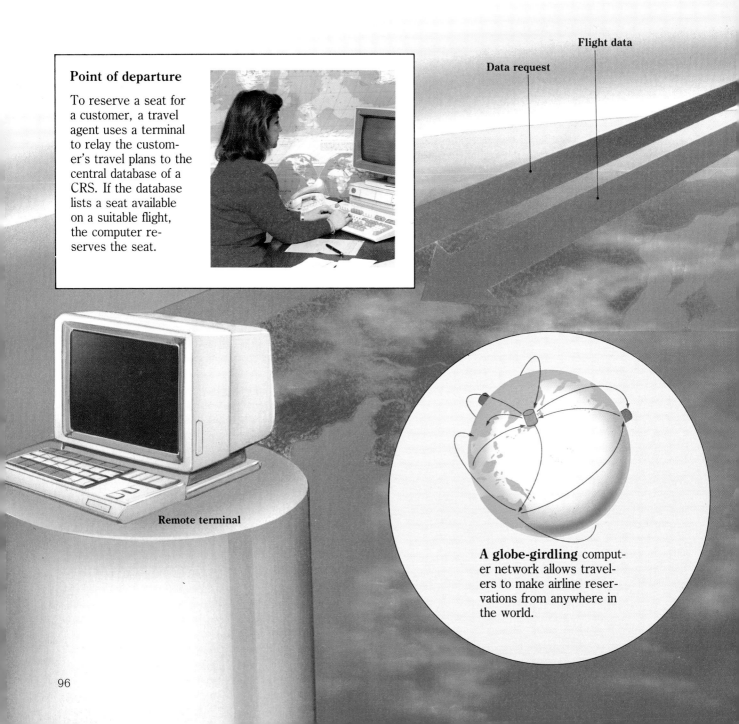

Point of departure

To reserve a seat for a customer, a travel agent uses a terminal to relay the customer's travel plans to the central database of a CRS. If the database lists a seat available on a suitable flight, the computer reserves the seat.

Data request

Flight data

Remote terminal

A globe-girdling computer network allows travelers to make airline reservations from anywhere in the world.

Inside an airline reservation system

At the heart of a computerized reservation system is a database that lists every available seat on every flight scheduled by an airline, as well as seat listings for the flights of other airlines. Whenever the CRS receives a request for a seat on a flight to a given destination, its central computer scans the database and provides a list of all flights with available seats; the computer also gives the price of each seat. If a traveler reserves a seat, the computer updates the database to show that the reserved seat is no longer available.

Airline A

Seat information

Airline B

Seat information

Airline C

Seat information

Mainframe computer

● A large-scale CRS

Conceived in the 1950s and first used in 1964 by American Airlines, the computerized reservation system has grown enormously ever since. Systems such as the American Airlines SABRE (for Semi-Automated Business Research Environment) and United Airlines' Apollo system are now worldwide in scope. So vast are the databases of these systems that large mainframes process the information they contain.

The CRS branches out

Enhancing the usefulness of the CRS, airline computers can now communicate with databases for hotel and rental car reservations. This lets a traveler secure an airplane seat, lodgings, and transportation with a single phone call.

A typical CRS screen display (*above*) lists the hotel reservations of a Japanese traveler en route to New York.

What Can a Robot Do?

The sort of robot typically seen in movies, with its humanoid form and comportment, has little in common with the robots being constructed in engineering laboratories around the world. The reasons for the disparity are twofold: The most efficient shape for a robot rarely resembles the human frame, and human behavior is much too complex to be captured in a computer program that could be used to direct the actions of a robot.

Engineers have succeeded, however, in building robots that mimic individual human functions. As shown below, mechanical hands called manipulators can grasp and rotate objects in much the same way that human hands do. And electronic eyes *(opposite)* enable robots to sense—and then interact with—their surroundings.

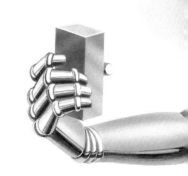

Automatons for every task

Sensor

Receiver

A robotic hand

A simple robotic hand, called a manipulator, consists of two fingers that open and close to grasp objects. Connected to pivoting joints, the manipulator can move objects up and down, and rotate them in all directions. An electronic sensor lets the manipulator's fingers monitor the strength of their grip.

Computer scientists have yet to create a fully functioning humanoid robot like the one shown below. Specialized robots, however, can imitate many limited human functions.

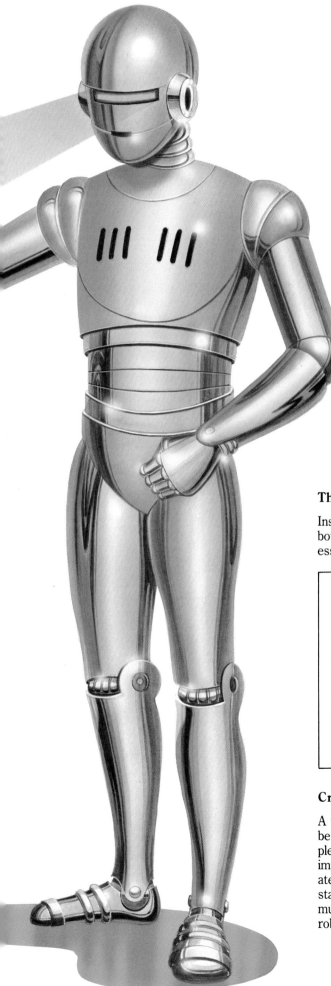

Digital vision

A robotic eye contains a television camera for recording visual images and a microprocessor for translating the images into digital signals.

As a robotic eye focuses on an object *(below)*, a microprocessor produces an electronic image *(right)*.

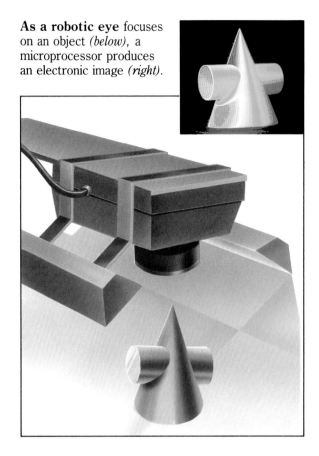

The soul of a machine

Instead of a brain, a computer program controls the actions of a robot. The program receives data from the robot's sensors, then processes the information to determine how the robot will respond.

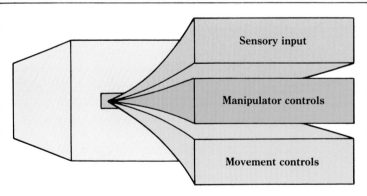

Sensory input

Manipulator controls

Movement controls

Crawl, don't run

A truly mobile robot remains to be built. Wheels provide the simplest means of movement but are impractical for robots that negotiate uneven surfaces, such as the staircase at right. One answer is multiple legs, which steady the robots on treacherous terrain.

How Do Robots Help Build Cars?

Nowhere in industry have robots had a more revolutionary impact than in the manufacture of cars. Robots usually outperform humans at the precise yet numbingly repetitive work of assembling an automobile.

On production lines, robots are used to stamp out and machine car parts, weld the parts together, paint them, install accessories, and transport components between work stations. Robots are even able to check their own work, using keen sensors to detect minute defects that might otherwise elude human eyes.

The use of robots has greatly boosted productivity in the automotive industry. Not only do the automatons work around the clock, but—when properly programmed—they rarely make mistakes. This enables automakers to produce cars faster and at lower cost.

Robots on the assembly line

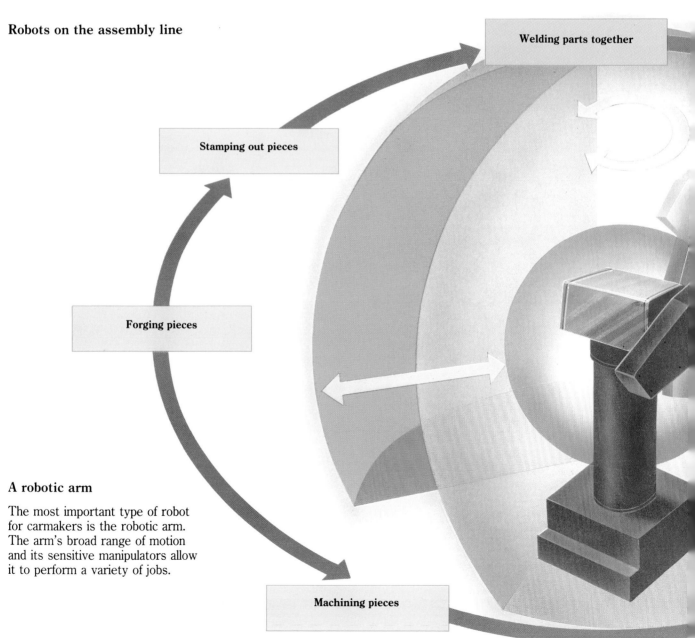

Welding parts together

Stamping out pieces

Forging pieces

Machining pieces

A robotic arm

The most important type of robot for carmakers is the robotic arm. The arm's broad range of motion and its sensitive manipulators allow it to perform a variety of jobs.

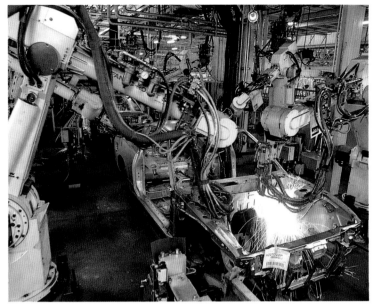

As the frames of partially assembled cars move along a production line, robotic arms reach in to weld the parts in place. Robots perform virtually all the welding required to make a car.

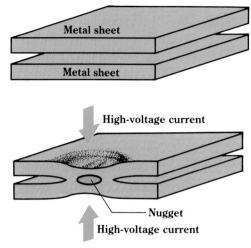

Spot welding is crucial to the manufacture of a car. Robotic arms press two pieces of metal together at a single spot; a strong electric current is then sent through the metal pieces, fusing them into a weld called a nugget.

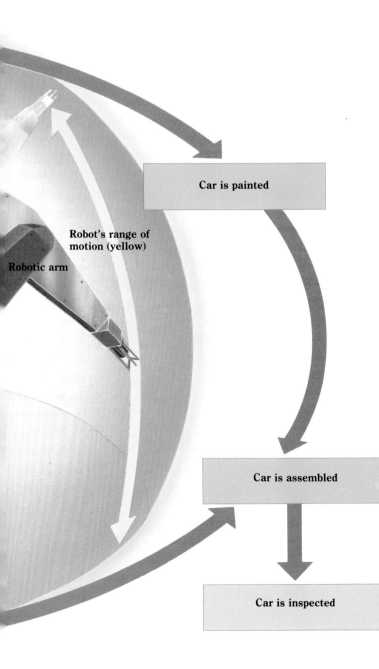

Car is painted

Robot's range of
motion (yellow)

Robotic arm

Car is assembled

Car is inspected

Car is shipped

Serving as programmable painters, two robotic arms cover a sports car with a uniform thickness of red paint from a precise angle and distance. The result is a near-perfect finish.

A robotic arm installs a windshield in a car nearing completion. Assembly robots like this one, which also fit tires and batteries in place, receive the necessary parts from transportation robots.

How Do Computers Work in Cars?

Computers have become a standard feature in nearly every automobile built today. On-board computers control vital aspects of a car's performance such as braking and steering. They also govern suspension, instrumentation, and engine efficiency. Computers built into cars cannot be operated by the driver or the riders; their programs are stored in read-only memory (ROM) and cannot be changed.

Computers were first installed in cars to reduce air pollution, when governments passed laws limiting the exhaust emissions from automobile engines. Sensors in the exhaust manifold analyze a car's emissions and transmit this information to a microprocessor. In turn, the microprocessor adjusts the engine's performance to reduce emissions and burn fuel more efficiently.

Sensors elsewhere in the car report data on the wheels, brakes, and suspension system to ensure a safe, smooth ride. Computers can make dozens of minor adjustments every second, continuously compensating for changing conditions. They prevent skids by sensing when the wheels are about to lock. In such a case the computer pumps the brakes to keep the wheels rotating. Computers help soften the jolts of a bumpy road by sensing pressure on the shock absorbers, then adjusting the tension to smooth out the ride. Computers also make possible innovations such as four-wheel steering and on-board navigation systems that tell drivers where they are and what the shortest route is to their destination.

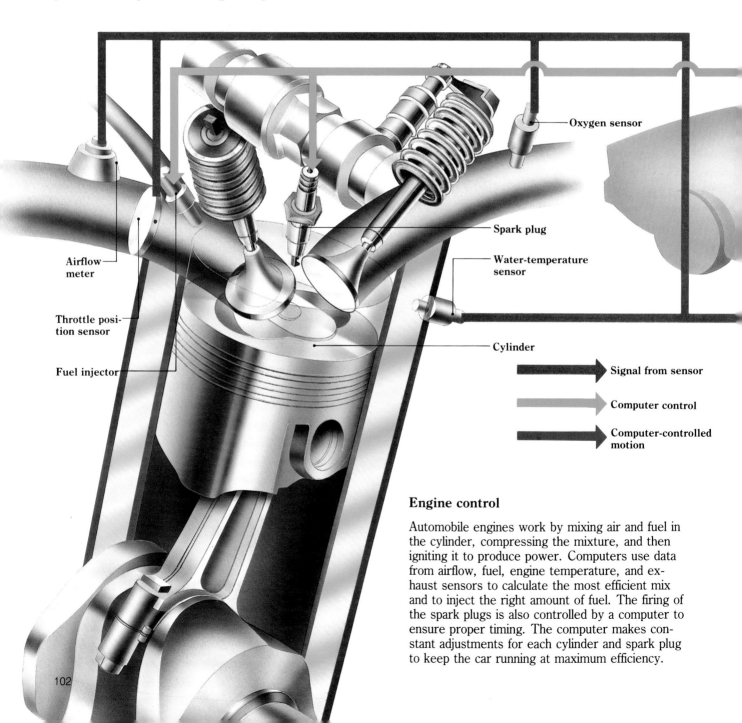

Oxygen sensor

Spark plug

Water-temperature sensor

Airflow meter

Throttle position sensor

Cylinder

Fuel injector

→ Signal from sensor

→ Computer control

→ Computer-controlled motion

Engine control

Automobile engines work by mixing air and fuel in the cylinder, compressing the mixture, and then igniting it to produce power. Computers use data from airflow, fuel, engine temperature, and exhaust sensors to calculate the most efficient mix and to inject the right amount of fuel. The firing of the spark plugs is also controlled by a computer to ensure proper timing. The computer makes constant adjustments for each cylinder and spark plug to keep the car running at maximum efficiency.

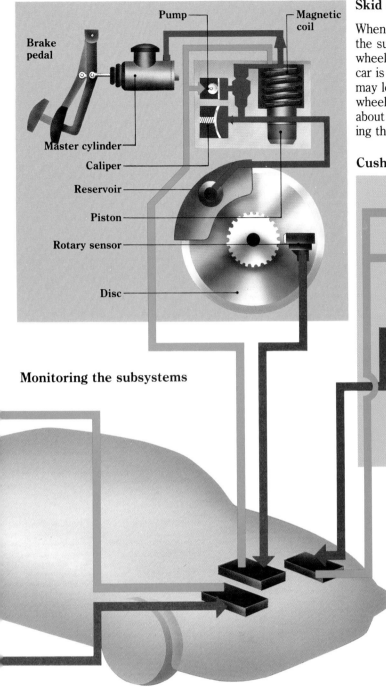

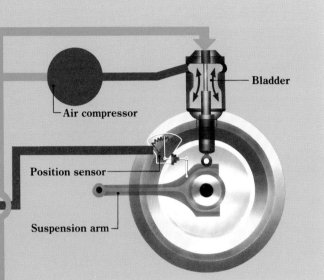

Skid control

When a driver slams on the brakes on a wet or icy road, the sudden pressure on the brakes can cause one or more wheels to lock—that is, to stop turning—even though the car is still moving. This eliminates traction, and the driver may lose control of the car. Rotation sensors detect a wheel about to lock. The computer pumps the brakes about 10 times a second, releasing the pressure and allowing the wheels to continue turning. This prevents a skid.

Cushioning the shocks

A car's weight is supported by the wheels, springs, and shock absorbers. The car's body sways with the vehicle's motion—the bumpier the road, the more the car bounces. Sensors report on the motion of the wheels' shock absorbers and adjust the amount of tension, or give, in each one to compensate for a rough road and provide a smooth, even ride for the passengers. When a car's load is unbalanced—when, for instance, the trunk is full—the computer pumps up the shocks where needed to keep the chassis level.

Instrument panel

Computer instrument displays give a car the look of a jet plane's cockpit. Needle gauges are being replaced by LCDs, or liquid crystal displays. "Heads-up" displays project data onto the windshield, freeing the driver to keep his or her eyes on the road.

On-board navigation system *(above)*

Digital instrument displays *(left)*

Can a Computer Run a House?

The growing use of computers in the home—from personal computers to microprocessor-driven alarm clocks—has inspired engineers to build dwellings whose every feature is controlled by a central computer. Such a smart house, as it is called, allows occupants to dictate how the home will be run in their absence. Before leaving for work, for example, a home-owner can instruct the master computer to videotape a television program at 3:00 p.m., begin warming dinner at 4:30, and turn on the heating or air conditioning at 5:00. These directions may also be delivered by phone.

A smart house offers cost savings as well as convenience. Linked to the local power company, a home's central computer can run energy-gobbling appliances when electricity rates are lowest. The computer can also choreograph the operation of all appliances that use hot water, such as the washing machine and dishwasher, to make the most economical use of the water heater.

Although the comfort and economy of a smart house offset its cost over the long run, such homes remain far more expensive than conventional abodes. As the price of the computer system decreases, however, smart houses may well become a familiar part of the landscape.

New chips on the block

Air conditioner

Master terminal

Fax machine

Monitor for data network

Audiovisual system

Telephone/answering machine

A data network

In a smart house, a central computer oversees the functioning of myriad information appliances—VCR, fax machine, telephone, security sensors. The central computer can be programmed from a master terminal or from a telephone.

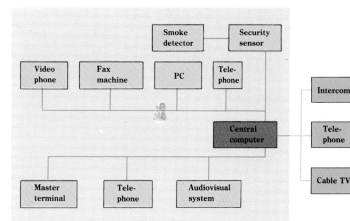

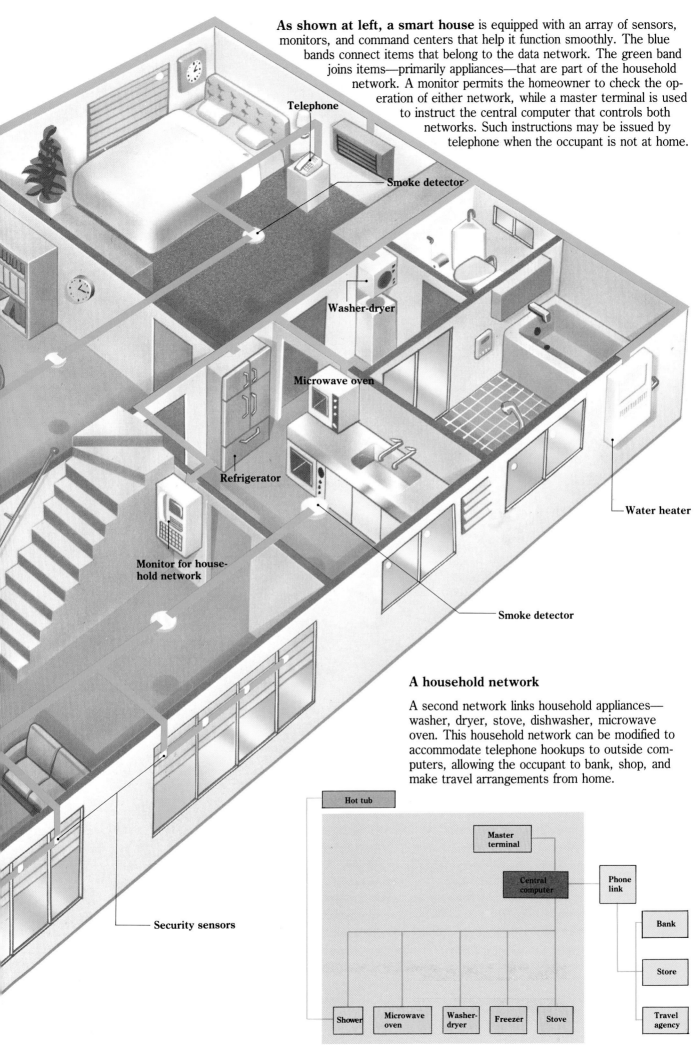

As shown at left, a smart house is equipped with an array of sensors, monitors, and command centers that help it function smoothly. The blue bands connect items that belong to the data network. The green band joins items—primarily appliances—that are part of the household network. A monitor permits the homeowner to check the operation of either network, while a master terminal is used to instruct the central computer that controls both networks. Such instructions may be issued by telephone when the occupant is not at home.

Telephone

Smoke detector

Washer-dryer

Microwave oven

Refrigerator

Water heater

Monitor for household network

Smoke detector

Security sensors

A household network

A second network links household appliances—washer, dryer, stove, dishwasher, microwave oven. This household network can be modified to accommodate telephone hookups to outside computers, allowing the occupant to bank, shop, and make travel arrangements from home.

Hot tub

Master terminal

Central computer

Phone link

Bank

Store

Travel agency

Shower

Microwave oven

Washer-dryer

Freezer

Stove

What Is Computer Crime?

Computer crime is the unauthorized alteration of—or simply access to—computer programs or data. In a society that is growing increasingly reliant on computers, computer crime is becoming an increasingly troublesome transgression.

Computer criminals have stolen millions of dollars from companies by unlawfully transferring funds out of computer accounts. Using virus programs that spread destruction from one computer to another, they have also crippled entire computer networks. Less harmful but equally vexing are computer "worms"—programs that replicate inside a system, consuming memory space until the computer has none to perform its assigned tasks.

Software engineers have designed a panoply of safeguards intended to combat these computer crimes. Most large computer systems, for example, require users to enter a password before they can gain access to a file. And some systems can even be ordered to protect themselves: Special programs record every attempt to gain access to the system and alert the operator to the presence of a virus.

Taking a byte out of crime

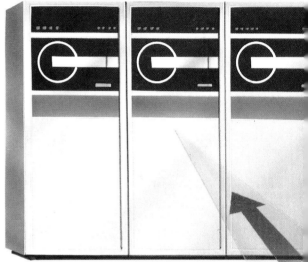

Computer system

Password

Most computer systems require the user to enter a password. If the password is valid, the computer grants access to the system; if not, access is denied. Complex computer security systems trigger an alarm if someone tries to use a fake password.

Of viruses and vaccines

A computer virus is a program that attacks a host program, forcing the computer to ignore the host and follow the instructions in the virus. Although some viruses instruct a computer merely to display a humorous message, others have erased entire databases. Once a virus enters a computer system, it can quickly infect other programs. To inoculate their machines against these programs, computer scientists have created "vaccine" programs that seek out the viruses and destroy them.

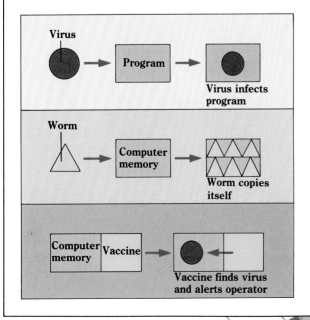

Virus → Program → Virus infects program

Worm → Computer memory → Worm copies itself

Computer memory / Vaccine → Vaccine finds virus and alerts operator

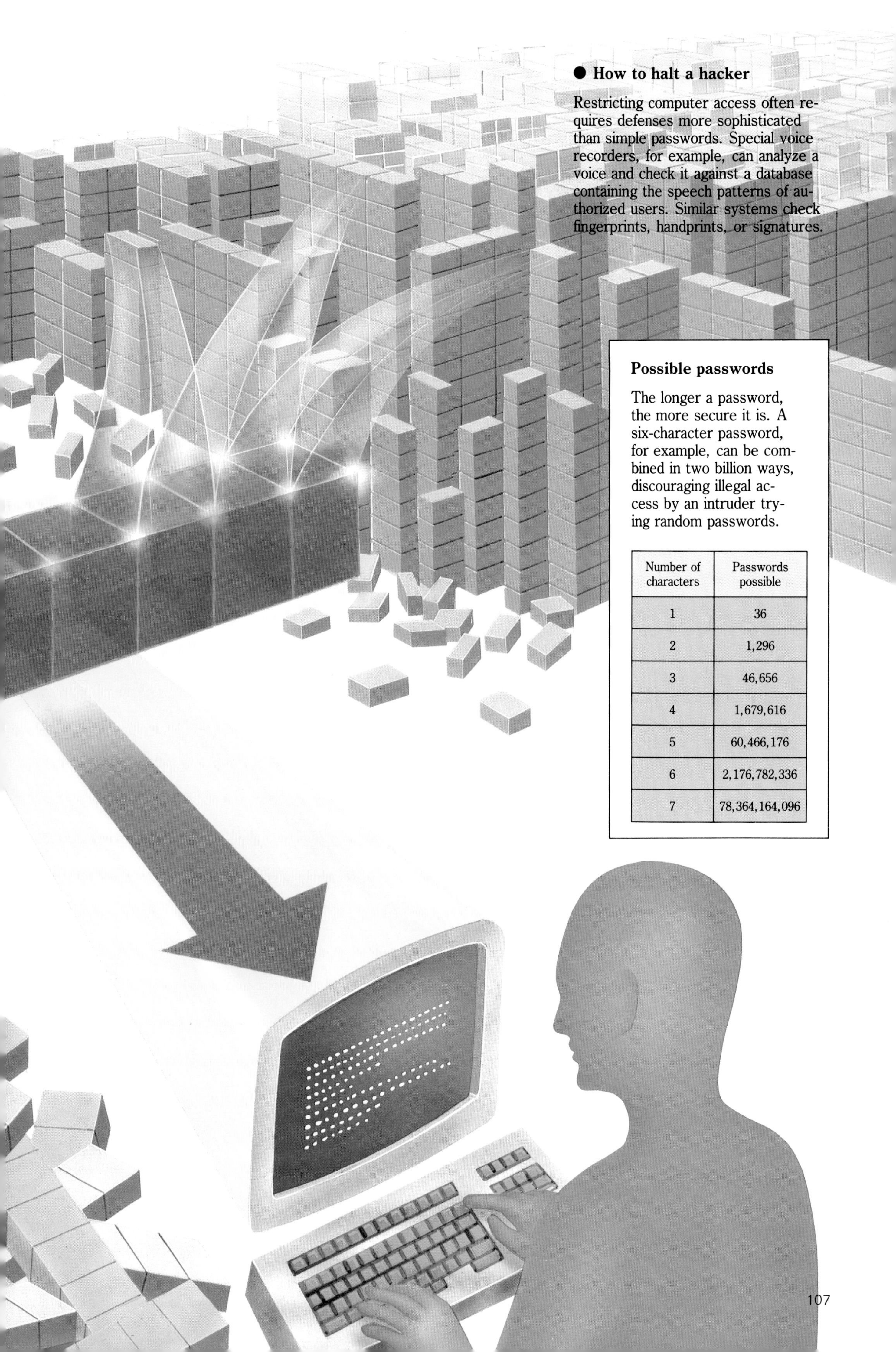

● How to halt a hacker

Restricting computer access often requires defenses more sophisticated than simple passwords. Special voice recorders, for example, can analyze a voice and check it against a database containing the speech patterns of authorized users. Similar systems check fingerprints, handprints, or signatures.

Possible passwords

The longer a password, the more secure it is. A six-character password, for example, can be combined in two billion ways, discouraging illegal access by an intruder trying random passwords.

Number of characters	Passwords possible
1	36
2	1,296
3	46,656
4	1,679,616
5	60,466,176
6	2,176,782,336
7	78,364,164,096

6
Computer Networks

Every computer has the unique ability to store massive amounts of information in a tiny space electronically. But the value of computers to businesses, researchers, governments, and individuals multiplies greatly when groups of computers are linked together into networks. Then, with blinding speed, data can be shared. Already, networked computers transmit voice messages, standard alphabetical or numerical texts, and digitized images over telephone lines. But a system slated to go on line promises to revolutionize telecommunications. Using the Integrated Services Digital Network, a person in New York will be able to sing "Happy Birthday" to a friend in Los Angeles, fax a photo of a bouquet of roses, and send a congratulatory note, all by plugging a computer into an outlet resembling an electrical socket and typing in a few commands.

An even faster sort of linkup called a local area network, or LAN for short, ties computers together with thin fiberoptic lines that transmit signals as rapid pulses of light. This way, small desktop computers can tap into larger mainframes to gain access to huge volumes of data. Teams of workers in different parts of a building, city, or state also can collaborate on a project, sending messages back and forth directly or by electronic mail. Soon people anywhere on the globe may be able to communicate through the wizardry of networked computers.

Like a giant spider web, phone lines spread over the planet, carrying voices across thousands of miles. One day, these same lines will also effortlessly transmit pictures and data between computers anywhere on the planet.

What Makes the Telephone Work?

When a person talks on the telephone, the voice can be heard as clearly as if that person were in the next room, even though he or she may be thousands of miles away. At one time, telephone voices often sounded distant, scratchy, and unclear. Occasionally, voices became scrambled, and callers found themselves talking to total strangers. Modern telephone systems seldom have these problems; they use computers to preserve the voice's quality and keep it separate from others. Computers accomplish this feat by changing a voice into a string of numbers and mixing it with thousands of others during its brief journey. A code identifies each voice and tells the telephone system's computers whose voice it is, where it is going, and what it sounds like. The code remains the same during the voice's travels. When a voice reaches its destination, it can be separated from other voices and will sound as clear as it did when it first entered the telephone.

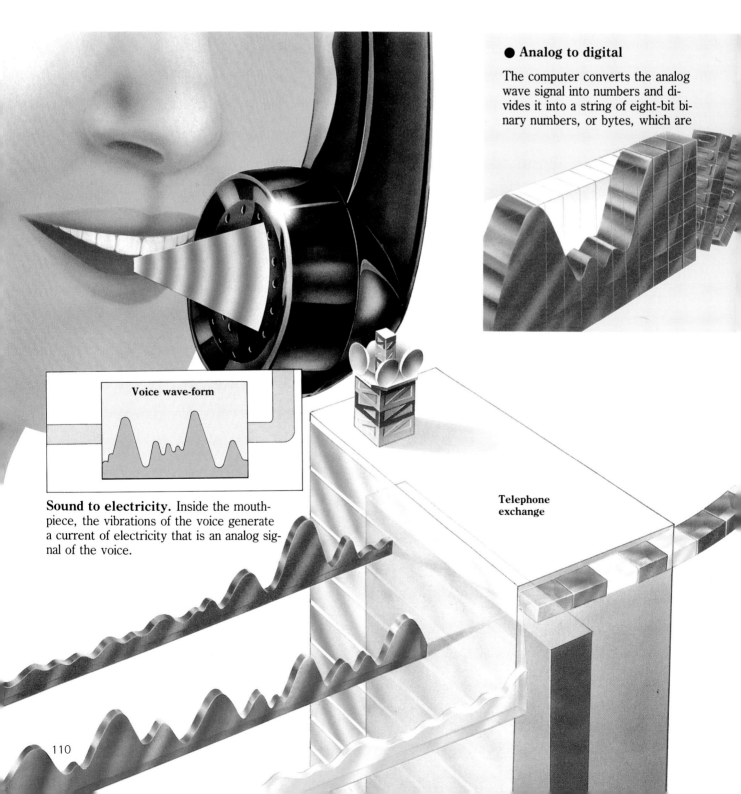

● **Analog to digital**

The computer converts the analog wave signal into numbers and divides it into a string of eight-bit binary numbers, or bytes, which are

Voice wave-form

Sound to electricity. Inside the mouthpiece, the vibrations of the voice generate a current of electricity that is an analog signal of the voice.

Telephone exchange

Digital to analog

The transducer in the telephone's receiver changes the voice back into sound waves.

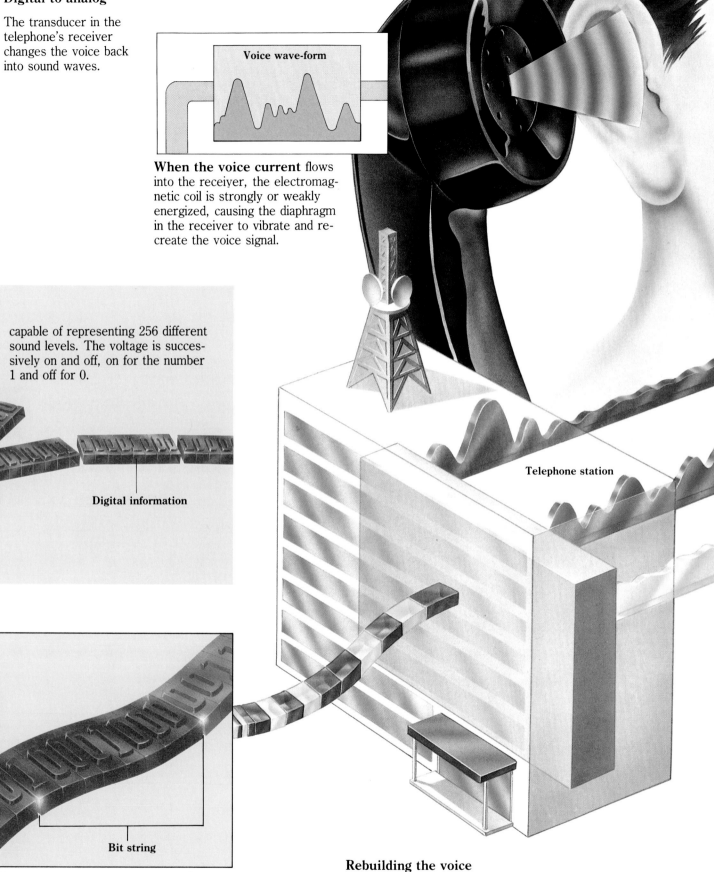

Voice wave-form

When the voice current flows into the receiver, the electromagnetic coil is strongly or weakly energized, causing the diaphragm in the receiver to vibrate and re-create the voice signal.

capable of representing 256 different sound levels. The voltage is successively on and off, on for the number 1 and off for 0.

Digital information

Telephone station

Bit string

Bit strings from many different voices are mixed in a single stream. Thousands of voices share a single telephone line without confusion.

Rebuilding the voice

The bit strings that made up the first voice *(red)* are separated from those of other voices. The telephone exchange picks them out of the stream and assembles them so that the voice can be rebuilt. Finally, the computer changes the digital signal back to an electrical analog signal.

What Is Teleconferencing?

Not long ago, if groups of people wanted to discuss something, they had to gather in one location. Now, by tapping into the technology of teleconferencing, people at far-flung locations can hold computerized versions of conference calls as easily as if they were all in the same room. In an audio teleconferencing system such as the one illustrated on these pages, microphones pick up the voices of people at two offices in different cities. Simple devices attached to either end of the phone line transform the sound waves of outgoing voices into digital impulses and translate incoming digital signals back into sound, which is then fed into a speaker for amplification. Special electronic circuits dampen both the echoes and the piercing squawks that normally result when sound from a speaker feeds back into a nearby microphone. A facsimile machine and an electronic sketchpad round out the equipment for the teleconference, so that illustrations and notes can be transmitted during the course of the meeting.

A two-way conference

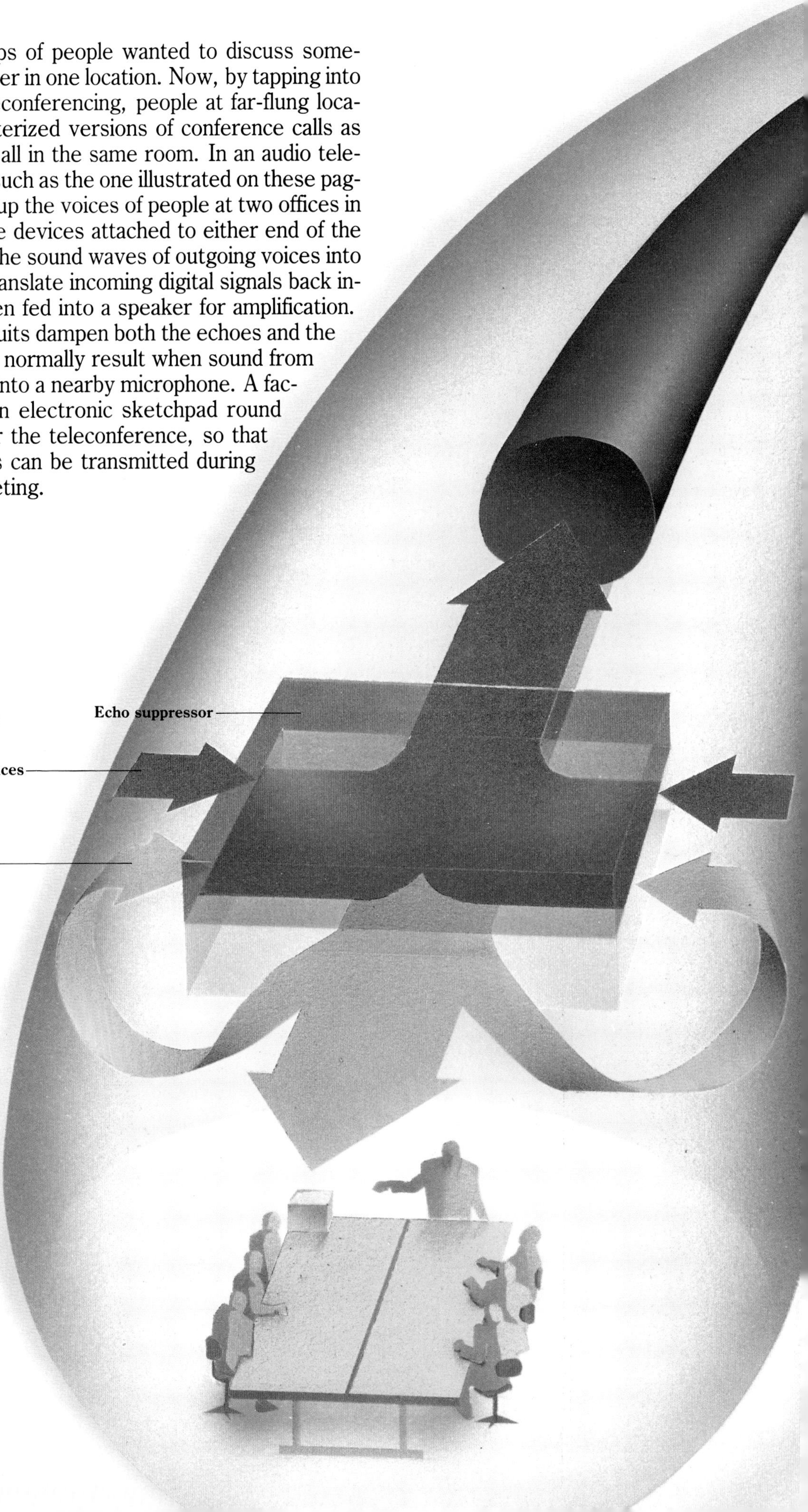

Echo suppressor

Voices

Sound from speakers

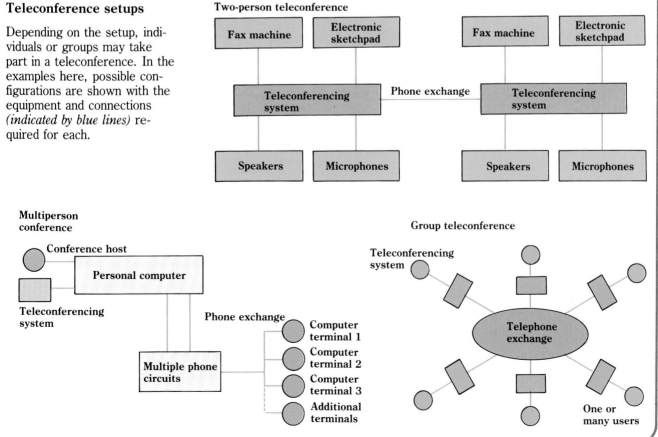

Phone exchange

Two-way phone line

With teleconferencing, companies can hold discussions without having to send their employees on expensive and tiring business trips. Or, students can take courses while living far away from colleges or universities. When they have questions for their teacher, they merely raise their hands—electronically—by typing into a personal computer. Already, many schools, corporations, and governments are taking advantage of the speed and ease of audio and computer teleconferencing. One day, specially designed rooms for videoconferencing, which now cost about $200,000 but are expected to become less expensive, may all but eliminate wasteful commuting and long-distance travel.

Teleconference setups

Depending on the setup, individuals or groups may take part in a teleconference. In the examples here, possible configurations are shown with the equipment and connections *(indicated by blue lines)* required for each.

Two-person teleconference

Fax machine	Electronic sketchpad		Fax machine	Electronic sketchpad

Teleconferencing system — Phone exchange — Teleconferencing system

Speakers	Microphones		Speakers	Microphones

Multiperson conference

Conference host

Personal computer

Teleconferencing system

Phone exchange

Multiple phone circuits

- Computer terminal 1
- Computer terminal 2
- Computer terminal 3
- Additional terminals

Group teleconference

Teleconferencing system

Telephone exchange

One or many users

How Are Illustrations, Text, and Photos Sent by Phone?

Facsimile, or fax, machines were invented in 1842 but only became popular in the late 1980s. They enable users to send photographs or pages of printed material over phone lines. Older analog fax machines deal strictly in black-and-white images, while newer digital versions capture shades of gray. Both types of machines first translate a visual image into a chain of information about the tone values of small segments called picture elements and then into corresponding electronic waves, which can travel over the phone lines. The transmission rate depends on the machine and density of material to be sent,

but it can be as fast as one page every three seconds. Upon reaching another fax machine, these waves are demodulated, or translated, back into a chain of information, which instructs a printer to produce an exact copy of the original image. Because of their ability to register gray tones by using a greater number of pixels, digital machines yield images far crisper and more detailed than those of analog faxes.

Faxing an image

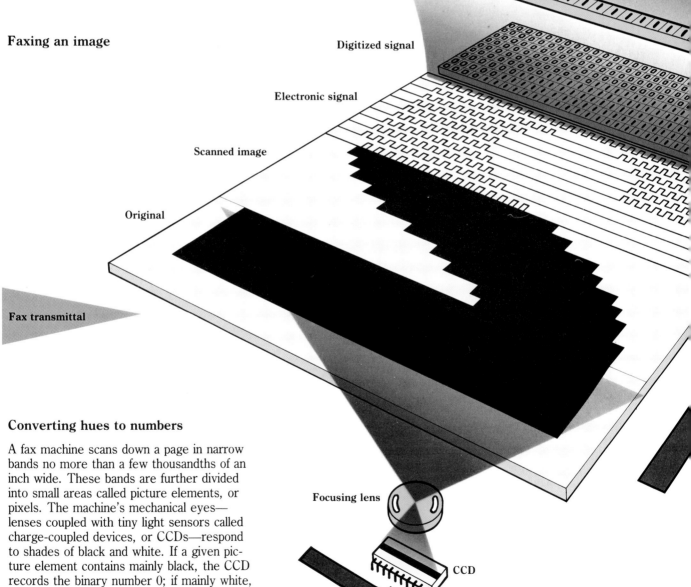

Encoding

Digitized signal

Electronic signal

Scanned image

Original

Fax transmittal

Focusing lens

CCD

Scanning direction

Converting hues to numbers

A fax machine scans down a page in narrow bands no more than a few thousandths of an inch wide. These bands are further divided into small areas called picture elements, or pixels. The machine's mechanical eyes—lenses coupled with tiny light sensors called charge-coupled devices, or CCDs—respond to shades of black and white. If a given picture element contains mainly black, the CCD records the binary number 0; if mainly white, the number 1. Each band of the image is thus converted into a string of 0s and 1s making up a digitized electronic signal.

Shrinking a digitized string

To speed transmission, the fax machine compresses, or encodes, the digital strings. In the one-dimensional coding method, the machine tallies clusters of 0s and 1s in each band. Two-dimensional coding involves comparing each band to the one above it and indicating which pixels remain the same and which have changed.

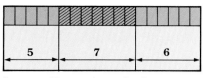

In one dimension, the fax machine reads this band as five white, seven black, and six white pixels.

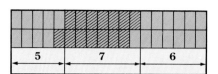

Encoding in two dimensions, the fax signals that the fifth pixel shifts to black, the twelfth to white.

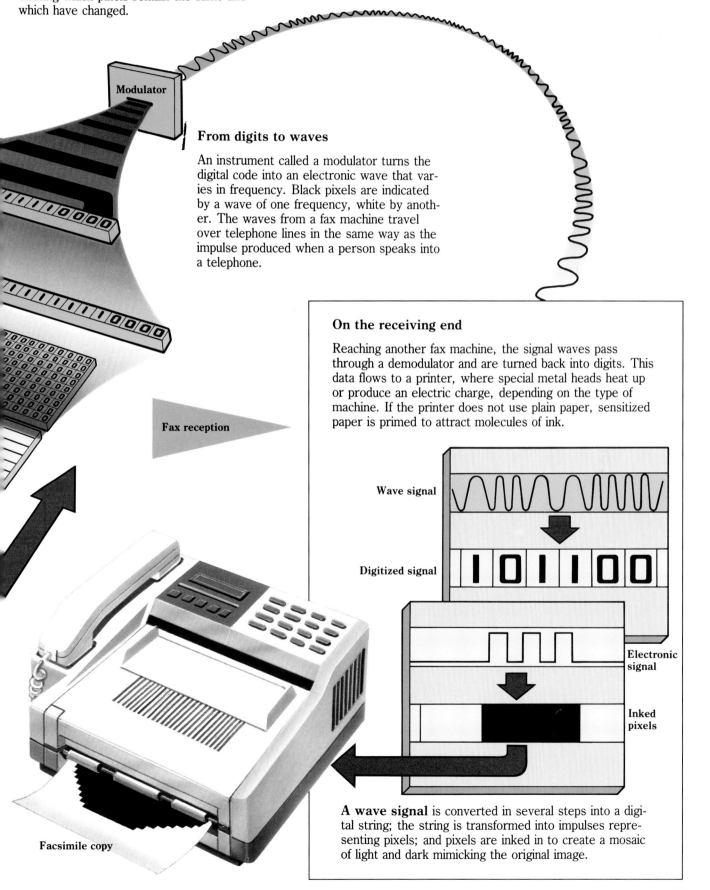

Modulator

From digits to waves

An instrument called a modulator turns the digital code into an electronic wave that varies in frequency. Black pixels are indicated by a wave of one frequency, white by another. The waves from a fax machine travel over telephone lines in the same way as the impulse produced when a person speaks into a telephone.

Fax reception

On the receiving end

Reaching another fax machine, the signal waves pass through a demodulator and are turned back into digits. This data flows to a printer, where special metal heads heat up or produce an electric charge, depending on the type of machine. If the printer does not use plain paper, sensitized paper is primed to attract molecules of ink.

Wave signal

Digitized signal

Electronic signal

Inked pixels

A wave signal is converted in several steps into a digital string; the string is transformed into impulses representing pixels; and pixels are inked in to create a mosaic of light and dark mimicking the original image.

Facsimile copy

What Is Electronic Mail?

Using electronic mail, or E-mail, is a way of rapidly sending data, documents, or recorded voice messages between personal computers or from one mainframe terminal to another. Incoming messages are filed in a recipient's "mailbox"—really a bank of magnetic memory disks—to be read immediately or left for later pickup. The millions of subscribers to the 60 or so commercial E-mail systems operating worldwide pay fees for the service. To send an electronic letter, a subscriber issues a few commands, and the computer's communications software posts messages accordingly through a modulator/demodulator, or modem. The messages travel over the phone lines to a designated mailbox. In similar fashion, a subscriber retrieves messages. Sometimes, faxes can also be delivered by E-mail. Electronic bulletin boards, considered a form of E-mail, let users post messages to one another, usually without charge. Readers can find an assortment of information and announcements, including handy software programs.

The brains behind E-mail

Computers hooked into an E-mail system send and receive messages according to the dictates of a master program called a message handling system, or MHS, stored in a system's central files.

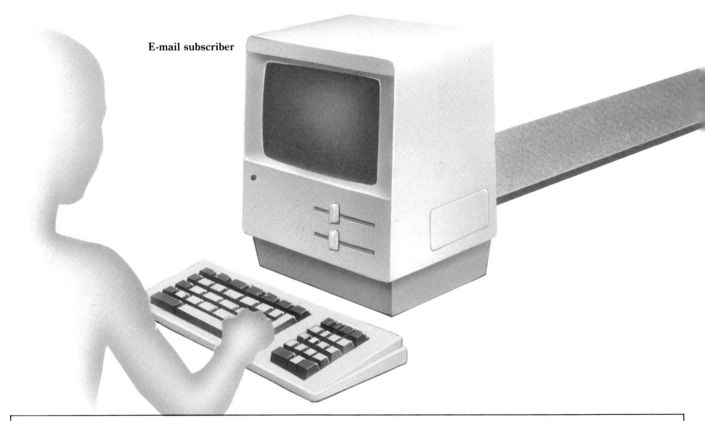

E-mail subscriber

The electronic mailmen

E-mail systems transmit and store messages electronically. With a few keystrokes, a message speeds from a remote terminal or PC to an E-mail system's mainframe. Then the message is routed automatically to a fax machine, which produces a hard copy, or paper printout, of it. The message may also be posted to a computer mailbox—really a designated file in a magnetic memory disk—from which it can be read, copied, or downloaded by the addressee.

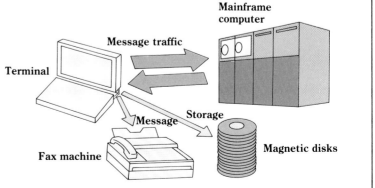

Mainframe computer

Message traffic

Terminal

Message

Storage

Fax machine

Magnetic disks

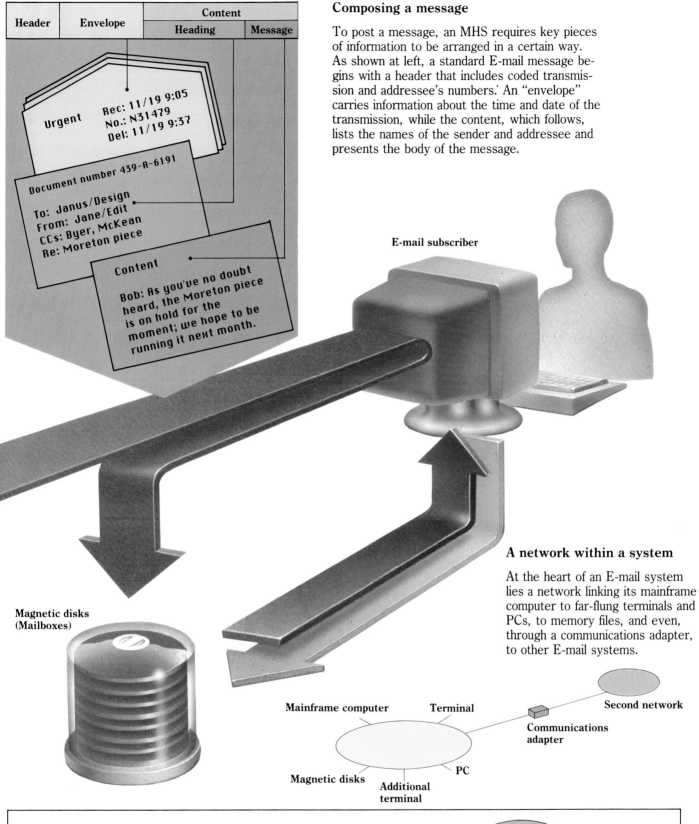

Header	Envelope	Content	
		Heading	Message

Urgent
Rec: 11/19 9:05
No.: N31479
Del: 11/19 9:37

Document number 439-A-6191

To: Janus/Design
From: Jane/Edit
CCs: Byer, McKean
Re: Moreton piece

Content

Bob: As you've no doubt heard, the Moreton piece is on hold for the moment; we hope to be running it next month.

Composing a message

To post a message, an MHS requires key pieces of information to be arranged in a certain way. As shown at left, a standard E-mail message begins with a header that includes coded transmission and addressee's numbers. An "envelope" carries information about the time and date of the transmission, while the content, which follows, lists the names of the sender and addressee and presents the body of the message.

E-mail subscriber

Magnetic disks
(Mailboxes)

A network within a system

At the heart of an E-mail system lies a network linking its mainframe computer to far-flung terminals and PCs, to memory files, and even, through a communications adapter, to other E-mail systems.

Mainframe computer
Terminal
Second network
Communications adapter
Magnetic disks
PC
Additional terminal

Electronic bulletin boards

In addition to sending E-mail messages, PCs armed with modems can tap into bulletin boards. Bulletin boards often are set up by a system operator using a single computer. By dialing a board's phone number and carrying out a simple log-on procedure, a person can gain access to messages from other computer users as well as leave messages for others.

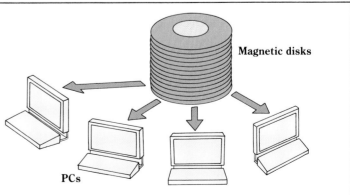

Magnetic disks

PCs

How Do Computers Transfer Data?

Data is stored inside a computer and moved around in digital form. This encoded data is dealt within eight-digit bundles of 0s and 1s called bytes. When two computers attempt to communicate, the handling of data becomes more complicated. Only identical types of computers are able to exchange data without altering its digital makeup. Computers from different manufacturers generally garble such unmodified messages. To further complicate matters, some telephone lines are unable to handle digital signals. Passing data through a modem solves these problems. Following certain rules, the modem converts the digital signal into an analog wave-form that can travel easily to different computers and over any kind of telephone line.

Shipping data in packets

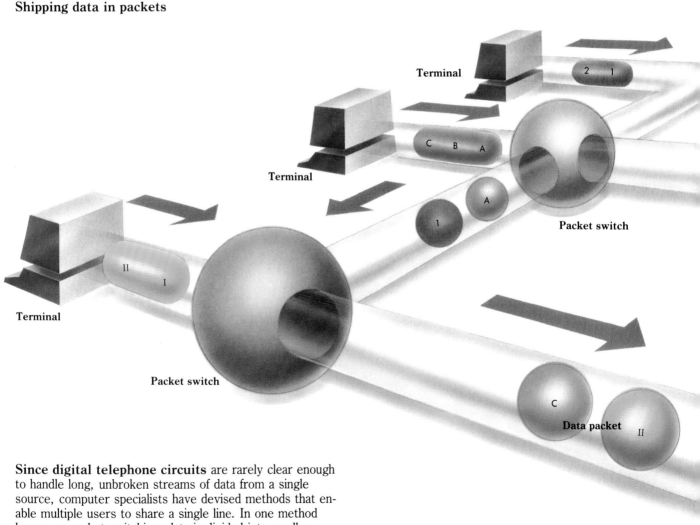

Terminal

Terminal

Terminal

Packet switch

Packet switch

Data packet

Since digital telephone circuits are rarely clear enough to handle long, unbroken streams of data from a single source, computer specialists have devised methods that enable multiple users to share a single line. In one method known as packet switching, data is divided into smaller chunks, called packets, and these chunks are labeled so that they can be quickly sorted out at the receiving end. The labels allow a computer to transmit packets in random order whenever space on a circuit becomes available. The system automatically routes the packets to the right computer on the receiving end, where the jumbled data is reordered.

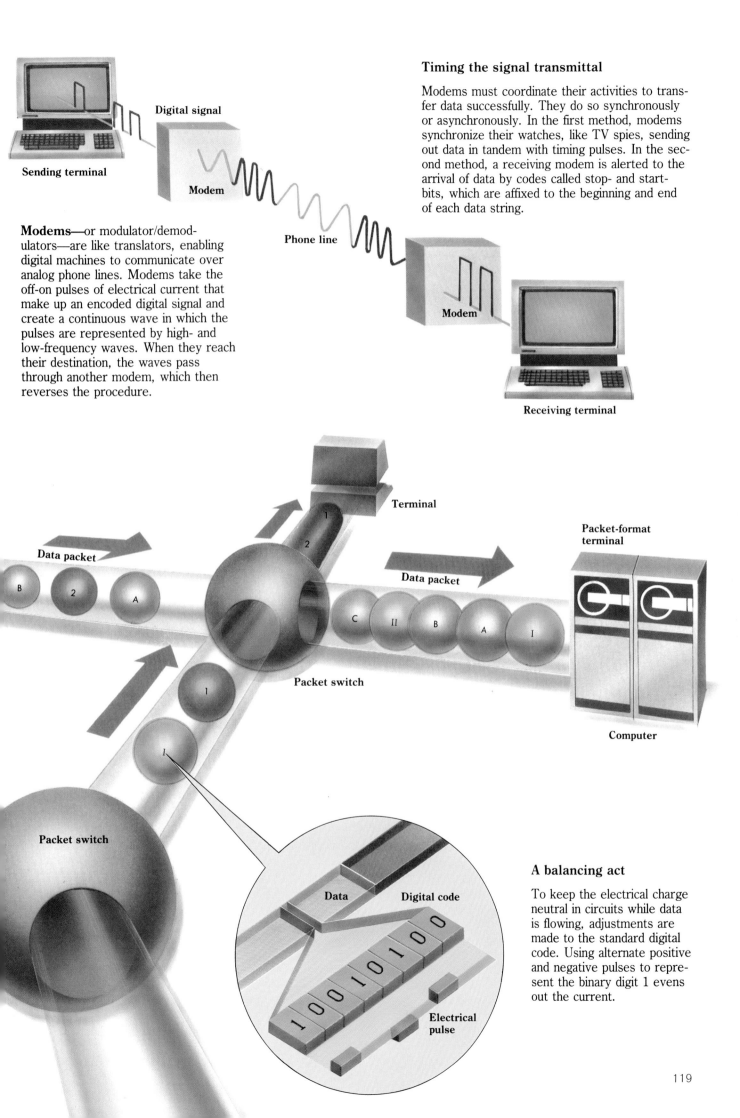

Digital signal

Sending terminal

Modem

Phone line

Modem

Timing the signal transmittal

Modems must coordinate their activities to transfer data successfully. They do so synchronously or asynchronously. In the first method, modems synchronize their watches, like TV spies, sending out data in tandem with timing pulses. In the second method, a receiving modem is alerted to the arrival of data by codes called stop- and start-bits, which are affixed to the beginning and end of each data string.

Modems—or modulator/demodulators—are like translators, enabling digital machines to communicate over analog phone lines. Modems take the off-on pulses of electrical current that make up an encoded digital signal and create a continuous wave in which the pulses are represented by high- and low-frequency waves. When they reach their destination, the waves pass through another modem, which then reverses the procedure.

Receiving terminal

Terminal

Data packet

Packet-format terminal

Data packet

Packet switch

Computer

Packet switch

Data

Digital code

Electrical pulse

1 0 0 1 0 1 0 0

A balancing act

To keep the electrical charge neutral in circuits while data is flowing, adjustments are made to the standard digital code. Using alternate positive and negative pulses to represent the binary digit 1 evens out the current.

Can Car Phones Work Anywhere?

To communicate, car phones—also called cellular phones—use radio waves rather than the wires of the standard phone system. In making a call from a car phone, a person first dials as usual. A radio message is thus sent to a base station operated by the cellular phone company. At the base station, which handles all calls within a given radius or zone, a circuit controller device assigns the call to a free radio channel. It also routes the signal to a second location, the cellular phone exchange office. By reading special codes emitted by the phone, the exchange office monitors the car's progress as it passes through the first base station's zone. If, during the call, the car happens to pass out of the first zone into another one, the exchange automatically diverts the call to a base station covering that zone. When a person calls a car phone, the caller is connected to the cellular exchange office. The office locates the car phone in question by radio, requests a free radio channel from the circuit controller, and makes a connection—via the base station—with the correct phone. The car phone then rings. When the driver picks it up, the circuit is completed.

■ **Making a cellular phone call**

Radio base station

● **The radio base station's job**

Each base station fields signals issued within 3 to 6 miles of it. To avoid interference, base stations with overlapping boundaries must use different frequency channels. But, even within the same city, stations far enough apart may use the same channel without difficulty.

● Place and channel

The cellular exchange pin-points the moving vehicle, while the circuit controller assigns it to a communications channel.

● The calling area

When a car strays beyond range of the most distant base station, the driver can no longer make cellular calls. If a call is under way when this happens, the signal will grow faint, then vanish.

Circuit controller

Covered zone

Cellular exchange office

Standard exchange office

Local phone systems that serve both homes and offices rely on wires that run underground or overhead and feed into exchange offices.

Passing calls between stations

During a mobile call, the cellular exchange office constantly monitors the position of the moving vehicle by checking the strength of the radio signal issuing from it. When the signal becomes too weak, the exchange alerts the base station, which in turn alerts a neighboring station to begin handling the call.

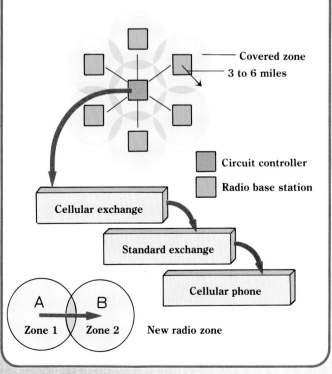

Covered zone
3 to 6 miles

Circuit controller

Radio base station

Cellular exchange

Standard exchange

Cellular phone

A
Zone 1

B
Zone 2

New radio zone

How Do Electronic Pagers Work?

Like cellular phones, electronic pagers receive and transmit messages by radio waves. A call to a paging device travels first to a base station, where it is analyzed and temporarily stored. Then, several base stations simultaneously radio the paging device, which will pick up the signal that is closest. In most cases, a pager begins to beep or vibrate when it receives a signal, thereby alerting a person to phone the base station for a message. These so-called tone-only pagers are gradually being replaced by message-display devices that include a small screen upon which telephone numbers and brief messages appear.

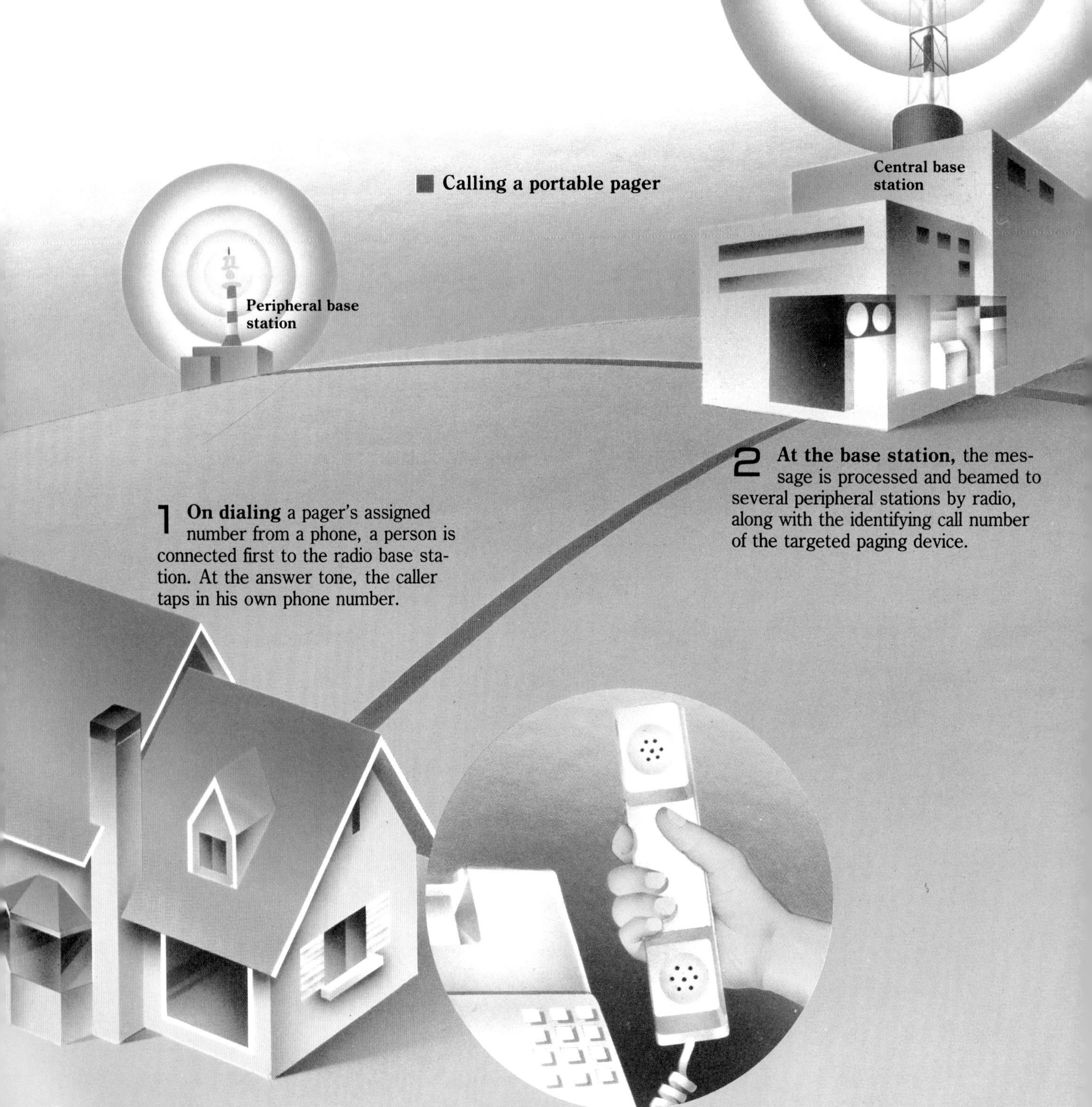

■ **Calling a portable pager**

Central base station

Peripheral base station

2 **At the base station,** the message is processed and beamed to several peripheral stations by radio, along with the identifying call number of the targeted paging device.

1 **On dialing** a pager's assigned number from a phone, a person is connected first to the radio base station. At the answer tone, the caller taps in his own phone number.

Anatomy of a call signal

Base stations repeat a signal every 20 seconds or so. To save battery power, paging devices are designed to recognize their own call numbers in just 1.4 seconds by being synchronized with the wave patterns emitted by the stations.

Approximately 20 seconds

1.4 seconds

Group 1	Group 2	Group 3		Group 15	Group 1	

Synchroniz-ing signal	Group designator	Call number 1	Call number 2		Call number 8

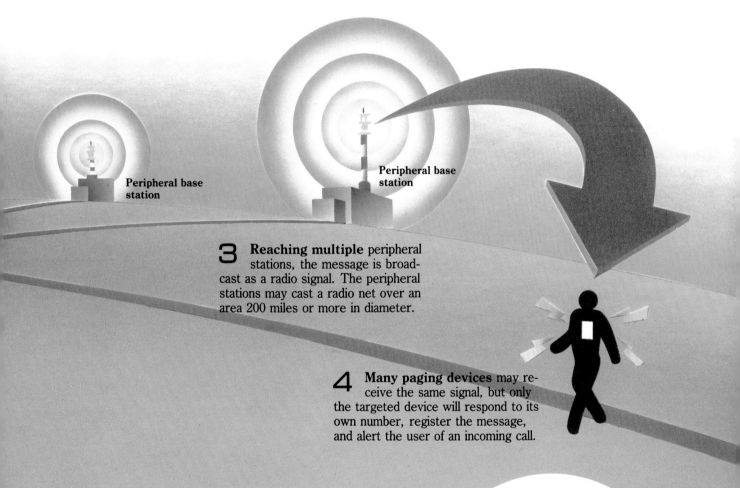

3 **Reaching multiple** peripheral stations, the message is broadcast as a radio signal. The peripheral stations may cast a radio net over an area 200 miles or more in diameter.

Peripheral base station

Peripheral base station

4 **Many paging devices** may receive the same signal, but only the targeted device will respond to its own number, register the message, and alert the user of an incoming call.

A paging device

The pager at right records and displays the number of the caller and also a few words. In the future, pagers will shrink in size. Some day, every digital wrist watch may double as a paging device.

The pager displays a short message.

Pager

How Are Messages Carried by Light?

Fiberoptic communication is a means of transmitting information over hundreds of miles using laser beams. Tiny glass fibers a few thousandths of an inch thick serve as guides for these beams of light. Inside the fibers, the waves of the laser beam speed along a central core of silica that is surrounded by an outer layer, called cladding. The cladding consists of a metal coating, bonded to a metal sheath that surrounds the silica core. This layer bends wayward waves back into the core, preventing their escape. So effective is the cladding that light passing along the fibers maintains a high degree of consistency and strength.

Thus noise—which means random, jumbled signals—is eliminated more completely than with conventional cables. Devices that boost and repeat the light signals need to be installed along fiberoptic cables only every 100 miles or so. Because of the cables' efficiency at maintaining accuracy, the transmission of off-on pulses of the laser beam, representing the standard binary code of 1s and 0s, can proceed swiftly. One of the latest transatlantic cables, made up of two pairs of optical fibers, is able to handle close to 300 megabytes of information per second, the equivalent of about 200,000 typewritten pages.

Fiber optics in action

Pulses of laser light issue from a semiconductor charged with electricity. They pass through a lens, travel along a fiberoptic cable, and are registered at the far end by a photodiode sensing device, which converts the signal into an electrical one that can be digitally deciphered.

Semiconductor
laser

Laser beam

Lens

Producing coded light pulses

When a strong-enough current passes through the semiconductor above, a beam of intense laser light is emitted. Turning this beam on and off at incredibly brief intervals of millionths of a second produces an oscillating wave. The highly regular oscillations serve to encode digital messages.

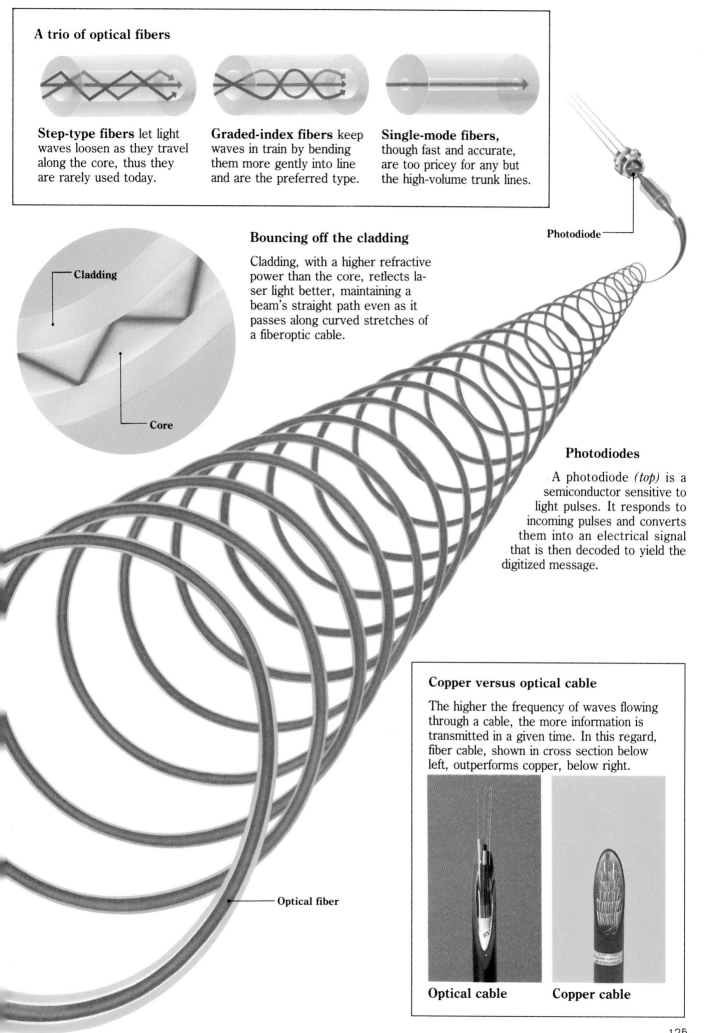

A trio of optical fibers

Step-type fibers let light waves loosen as they travel along the core, thus they are rarely used today.

Graded-index fibers keep waves in train by bending them more gently into line and are the preferred type.

Single-mode fibers, though fast and accurate, are too pricey for any but the high-volume trunk lines.

Photodiode

Bouncing off the cladding

Cladding, with a higher refractive power than the core, reflects laser light better, maintaining a beam's straight path even as it passes along curved stretches of a fiberoptic cable.

Cladding

Core

Photodiodes

A photodiode *(top)* is a semiconductor sensitive to light pulses. It responds to incoming pulses and converts them into an electrical signal that is then decoded to yield the digitized message.

Optical fiber

Copper versus optical cable

The higher the frequency of waves flowing through a cable, the more information is transmitted in a given time. In this regard, fiber cable, shown in cross section below left, outperforms copper, below right.

Optical cable   **Copper cable**

How Do Picture Phones Operate?

Picture phones, also known as videophones, enable distant parties to see one another as they speak. Prototypes introduced at the 1964 World's Fair in New York kindled the imagination, but the technology did not actually become affordable until the mid-1980s. Today, the key to the system is a large, boxlike item called a codec, for coder/decoder, which digitizes video images, pares down that information to a minimum using a technique called band compression, and transmits the resulting data over a phone line. A codec at the other end reverses the steps to produce either still or moving images. The realism of these images depends in part on the frequency with which the codec samples the video feed and transmits it. The more often the sampling, the smoother the movements appear on the receiving end. But, since video images are made up of some 90 million different bits of information per second, and phone lines transmit only a fraction of that amount, videophone images will remain somewhat blurry and jerky until better processing techniques are developed.

A new, compact videophone model sends full-color images over the lines.

Images traveling by phone

● Limiting the number of frames

A standard TV signal transmits 30 frames a second—far more than can travel over the phone lines. Videophones work with about 10 frames per second, edited down by the codec, which mainly deletes repetitive frames.

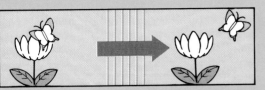

First image   Editing   Second image

Still-image videophones

Regular phone lines carry limited amounts of information, thus videophones installed in homes are able to transmit only still images. They send about one snapshotlike image every 6 to 10 seconds, during which time the phone line is fully occupied and conversation must come to a complete stop.

A typical videophone, shown at left, has a small screen atop which is mounted a video camera to film the person making the call. While the largest proportion of the digitized information making up each call is devoted to image and voice, the phone also adds codes to help eliminate errors in transmission that would produce interference on the other end.

● Making do with less

Digitized images are broken down into picture elements, or pixels. Realistic TV images contain as many as 10 times more pixels than the pictures produced by a still-image videophone.

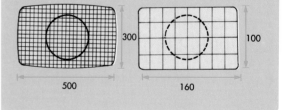

● From several images to a few

To compress the amount of data to be conveyed, the codec scans a frame and, by complicated mathematical reasoning, predicts whether the next frame will appear the same. If it guesses incorrectly, feedback alerts the codec, which will then include data about the change in its next signal. Other mathematical techniques also are used, but all winnow excess data and reduce the time spent sending images over the phone line.

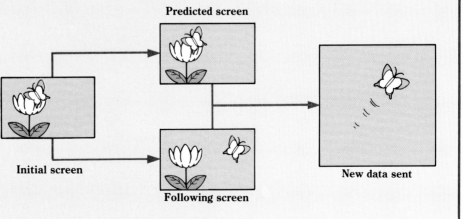

Predicted screen

Initial screen

Following screen

New data sent

How Do Orbiting Satellites Aid Global Communications?

Rocketed into space, most communications satellites settle into geostationary orbits; that is, they fly at the same speed as the earth rotates and so appear in fixed position with respect to the ground. Circling at 22,300 miles above the equator, one such satellite can monitor radio signals across a third of the planet. Covering the entire globe requires only three satellites. Early satellites, like the U.S. Echo lofted into orbit in 1960, merely reflected radio signals beamed up to them. Advanced versions not only pick up signals, but also amplify and retransmit them to precise locations on the ground. Since the launch of the first commercial communications satellite, INTELSAT I in 1965, the devices have become increasingly sophisticated. The latest solar-powered satellites juggle 30,000 phone calls or four TV transmissions at the same time. The various signals are beamed up by towering antennas at uplink stations and fielded by a satellite's transponder. This electronic instrument boosts a signal and switches it to an antenna, which transmits to the appropriate downlink station. In order to prevent interference, the uplink and downlink signals are relayed over different frequencies.

● **Spanning the globe**

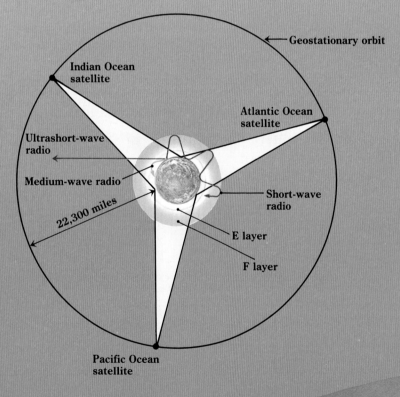

- Geostationary orbit
- Indian Ocean satellite
- Atlantic Ocean satellite
- Ultrashort-wave radio
- Medium-wave radio
- Short-wave radio
- 22,300 miles
- E layer
- F layer
- Pacific Ocean satellite

Arrayed in geostationary orbits, a trio of INTELSAT satellites *(left)* enable the worldwide transmission of long-wave radio signals. Handling the regions surrounding the Pacific, Indian, and Atlantic ocean basins, the satellites make high-speed telephone, television, and telegraph communications possible. Radio signals in the HF (high-frequency) range fail in this regard, because they bounce off charged particles blanketing the atmosphere in bands known as the E and F layers.

● **Downlink antenna**

This parabolic antenna can pick up even faint satellite signals. Most downlinks also serve interchangeably as uplink antennas.

- Primary emitter
- Reflector
- Secondary reflector

1. Solar-cell array
2. Parabolic reflector
3. Parabolic reflector
4. Parabolic reflector
5. Parabolic reflector

An orbiting antenna

Like earthbound antennas, this satellite version consists of a pronglike device called the primary emitter and a reflecting parabolic shield. The two elements work together to capture incoming radio waves and to eliminate any scattering of outgoing waves.

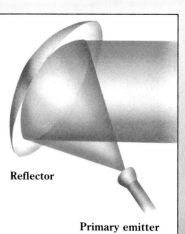

Reflector

Primary emitter

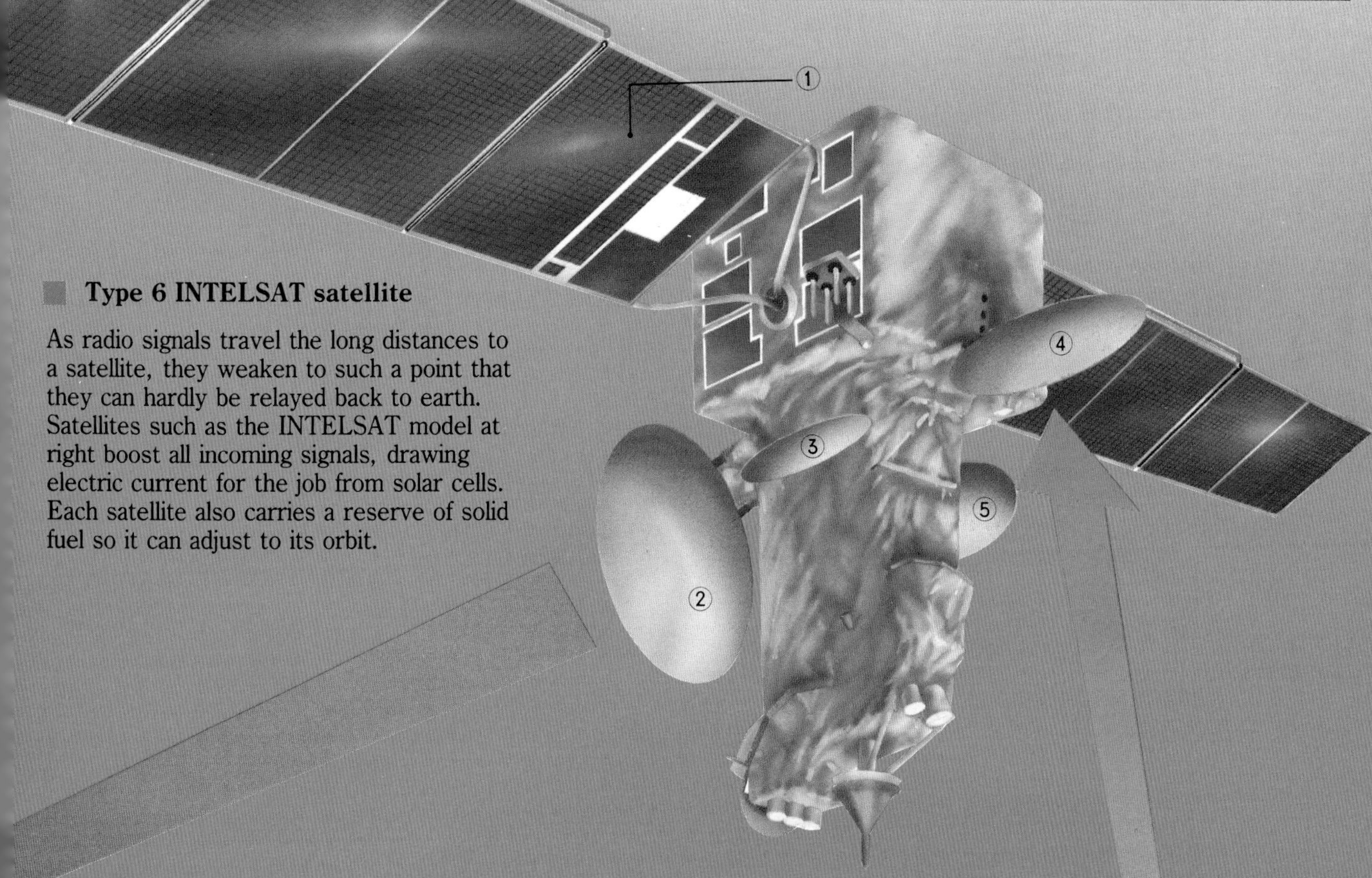

Type 6 INTELSAT satellite

As radio signals travel the long distances to a satellite, they weaken to such a point that they can hardly be relayed back to earth. Satellites such as the INTELSAT model at right boost all incoming signals, drawing electric current for the job from solar cells. Each satellite also carries a reserve of solid fuel so it can adjust to its orbit.

Ground stations

Stations around the globe carry on business with INTELSAT satellites via huge, 30-foot-wide parabolic antennas, such as the one shown at left.

7
Science and Computers

Computers are as commonplace as typewriters in modern society, performing astonishing feats in the service of science. Computers turn a spacecraft's cameras toward Neptune; implanted in miniature form under the human skin, a computer can control the rhythm of the heart. A computer can help a golfer perfect a swing or guide a missile on its deadly path.

One of the most useful ways that computers help researchers is by running simulations—models of changeable, real-life phenomena. Scientists began to use them this way soon after World War II, when they needed to test aircraft and missiles without using (and destroying) the real things. Simulations are now used in the fields of chemistry, biology, medicine, and automobile and ship engineering, and in the development of optical and acoustic systems, and more. No computer can exactly duplicate actual conditions, but they can help people understand and provide solutions to some of the problems of everyday life.

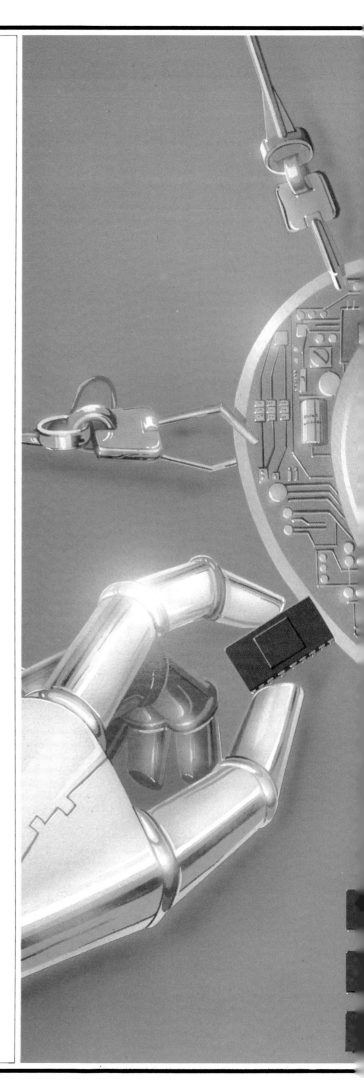

Although no computer has yet made a heart for itself, computers are being used to build other machines—on the auto assembly line, for instance.

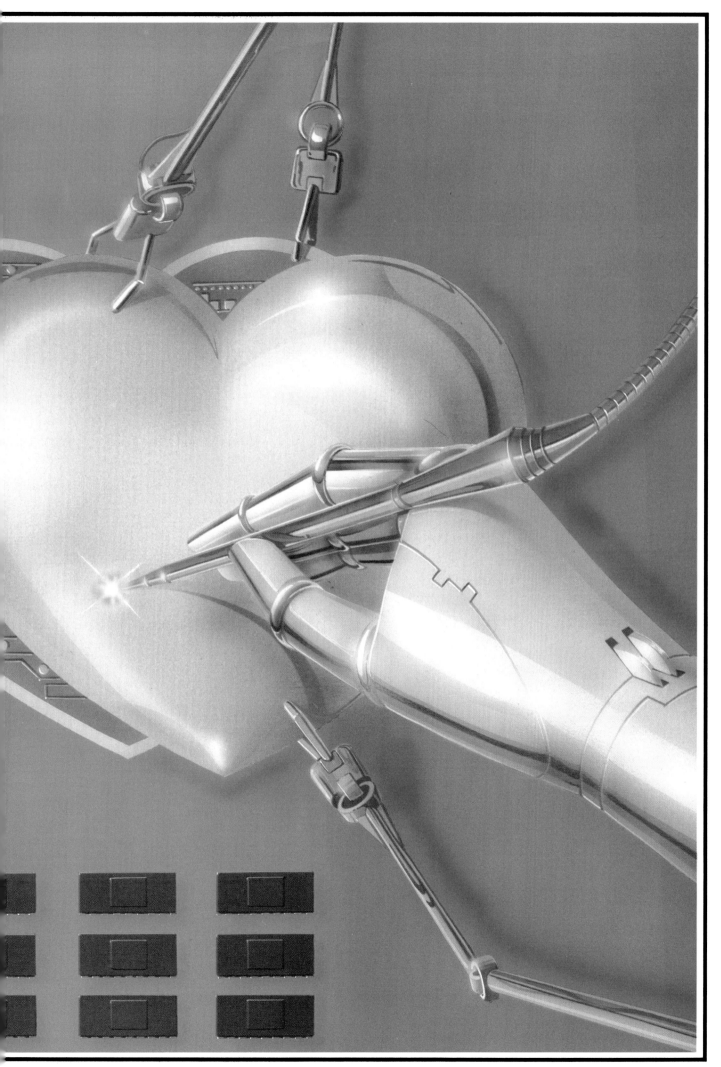

What Is a Computer Model?

Before computers were commonly used, engineers and designers constructed small, three-dimensional versions of whatever project they were developing. That way, they could tinker with a model without going to the expense of experimenting with the real thing. Now researchers can build models within computers—sending information into the machine and creating an easily manipulated simulation on the screen.

With computers, engineers can, for example, improve traffic patterns. To find out how to improve the timing of traffic lights and prevent traffic jams, engineers first learn what is happening on real streets. Using sensors under the road, plus recording devices, the engineers find out how many cars typically pass through each intersection in a particular time period, how many generally turn left or right, and so on *(below)*. Then they feed this information into the computer in digital form, creating a model of the streets, cars, and intersections. Now the engineers can experiment with different traffic-light sequences in the computer simulation. Eventually, the model will allow them to determine how best to set traffic lights at real intersections.

Car watching

Wire sensors buried about an inch and a half beneath each lane of a busy road note every car and truck approaching an intersection. This information moves on to a local control cabinet *(far left)* to be organized by a microprocessor. The data will help researchers understand the volume and direction of traffic on the roads. It can also be fed into a central traffic-control computer, which will adjust traffic lights accordingly.

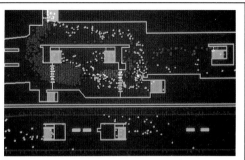

Passengers *(red)* leave the station.

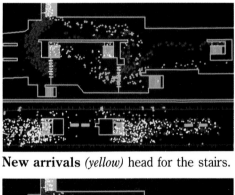

New arrivals *(yellow)* head for the stairs.

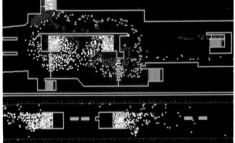

Arrivals pass through turnstiles.

How to keep a crowd moving

To find out how to design an efficient train station, designers feed information into a computer detailing how many people get on and off trains and where they go within the station. Then the designers create a model that simulates the arrival of trains at different intervals, with arriving and departing passengers coded by color in the simulation. This model shows the builders where best to locate stairs, turnstiles, entrance corridors, and other station features. The structure that results consists of two levels connected by two central staircases, with turnstiles located on the upper floor.

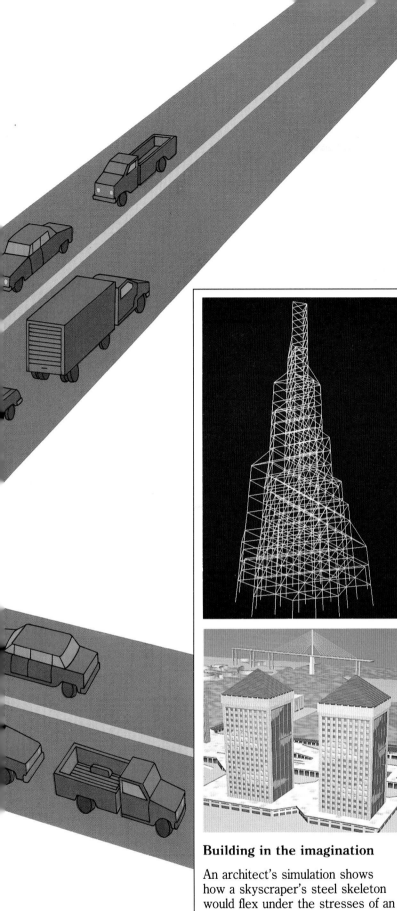

Building in the imagination

An architect's simulation shows how a skyscraper's steel skeleton would flex under the stresses of an earthquake *(top)*. A more realistic-looking model allows a designer to assess the impact of two new buildings along a shoreline *(bottom)*.

Can Computers Predict the Weather?

Predicting the weather seems like an everyday activity. However, predicting it accurately for longer than a few hours ahead, or for more than a small area, is fiendishly difficult. The atmosphere is a huge, fluid region in which winds, temperatures, atmospheric pressure, and many other factors constantly interact. Because of this, meteorologists (scientists who study weather) use some of the most powerful computers in the world to help make their calculations.

Using a system of grid lines, meteorologists divide the atmosphere into hundreds of three-dimensional segments. They observe and record such conditions as wind direction, temperature, atmospheric pressure, and water vapor in each segment. Then using the existing conditions, the meteorologists compute what the weather will be an hour or a day later based on the probable rate of change. Even on supercomputers, such programs can take hours to run.

**Grid model for
Earth's atmosphere**

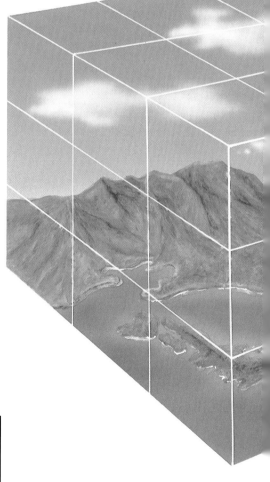

Watching the weather

Scientists collect information on the weather from stations on land, on sea, and even in space.

1. Meteorological rocket
2. Weather satellite
3. Surface weather station
4. Radar station
5. Maritime station

Storm within a computer

Modeled by a powerful supercomputer, a severe thunderstorm looms over an artificial landscape. Colored balls show the movement of air in and around the storm.

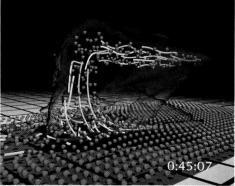

0:45:07

Piecing together a prediction

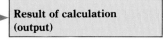

```
┌─────────────────────────┐      ┌─────────────────────┐
│ Observed data such as    │ ──→  │ Result of calculation│
│ temperature and          │      │ (output)             │
│ precipitation            │      └─────────────────────┘
└─────────────────────────┘
            │
            ↓
┌─────────────────────────┐
│ Estimated rate of change │
│ in each observed segment │
└─────────────────────────┘
            │
            ↓
┌─────────────────────────┐
│ How conditions will spread│
│ to other segments         │
└─────────────────────────┘
            │
            ↓
┌─────────────────────────┐
│ Changes in temperature   │
│ and relative humidity    │
└─────────────────────────┘
```

A weather prediction results from an analysis of calculated values stored in the computer. As information about different conditions is entered, each new computer calculation affects the next one. The results of the calculations are then represented graphically as a weather forecast map.

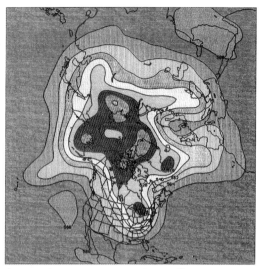

A weather map of the United States

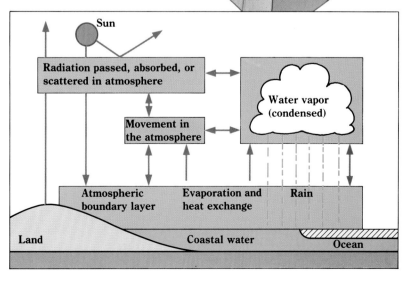

The elements of weather

Because the weather is affected by so many different variables, the equations that go into weather forecasts are difficult to solve. Variables for any segment on a weather grid include, among other things, the amount of radiation from the sun, the reflection of radiation by land surfaces, heat exchanged between the atmosphere and the sea or the land below, and evaporation and condensation of moisture.

Why Are Computers Used in Sports?

For athletes who want to get the most out of their skills, computers are becoming valuable tools. Motion analysis programs can now show people how to change their movements to improve their performance. They can also demonstrate the different ways a ball flies through the air, depending on how it is hit.

The key to these programs is computer modeling. For instance, a coach might take motion pictures of an athlete performing a sport—say, ski jumping or diving. This information is used to help construct a computer model of the movements. Many times, the computer models take the form of stick figures on a computer screen; various points of the body such as shoulders, el-

bows, hips, and knees are connected with lines.

The computer user then asks the program to move each of these body parts at different speeds and accelerations to find out which movements taken in which order would create the overall best result—for instance, in launching the body off a ski jump's ramp.

Models to display the motion of balls in the air are similar. Once the programmer has put the basic information into the computer, the model is able to run through different simulated forces to determine how the ball will fly and bounce under different conditions.

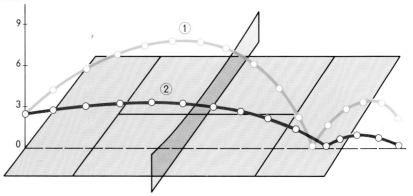

Steps to high performance

Motion analysis on the computer has several steps. First, someone films an athlete in action. Then a stick figure mimics the motions on a computer screen. Programmers can see what motions will improve performance.

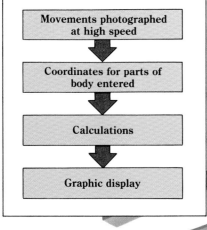

Movements photographed at high speed

↓

Coordinates for parts of body entered

↓

Calculations

↓

Graphic display

The flight of a tennis ball

At right, a computer model simulates the paths of a tennis ball hit with the same force but with two different spins. Path 1 shows how a tennis ball would travel and bounce if hit with a topspin; path 2 shows how it would react to a backspin. The ball position is shown at 0.1-second intervals.

Analysis of a ski jump

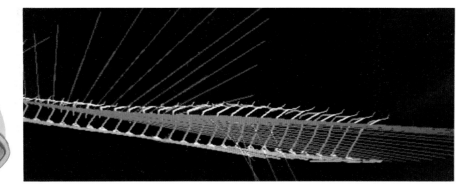

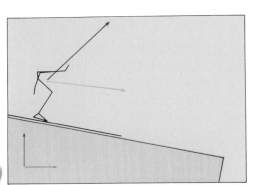

1 Maximum acceleration

Reduced to a stick figure by a motion analysis program, a skier takes off from a ski jump *(above)*. The red lines show the direction and acceleration of the skier's center of gravity; the blue lines show the level and direction of the skier's velocity.

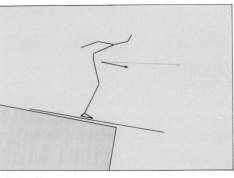

2 Takeoff

Capturing moments

Plucked from a motion analysis display, these three stick-figure frames isolate distinct parts of a skier's jump. The first shows the position at which the skier is thrusting upward to the greatest extent; the second, at the very end of the jump ramp, displays the position at which the skier is thrusting forward to the greatest extent; and the third shows the skier in flight. As above, the red lines show the direction of the skier's center of gravity; blue lines show the direction of velocity.

3 In flight

Perfecting a golf swing

To gather information for a sports analysis program, the golfer at the far right and his club and ball are all outfitted with sensors hooked up to a computer. As the golfer swings his club, information on his movements passes to the computer and eventually will be plotted on the screen.

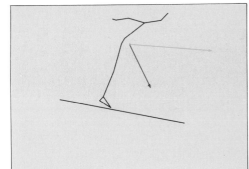

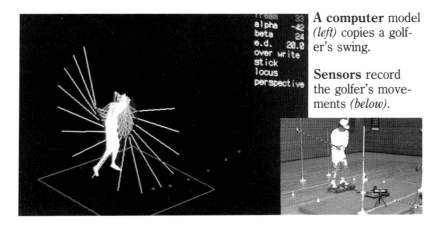

A computer model *(left)* copies a golfer's swing.

Sensors record the golfer's movements *(below)*.

How Can Computers Help the Body?

The field known as biomedical engineering—which uses technology to help solve medical problems—has been revolutionized by the computer chip. Because computers have become so small, they can fit inside artificial limbs or organs to help them move, pump blood, or otherwise work to keep a person healthy.

Computers inside artificial legs and arms sense and react to muscle movements in the flesh to which they are attached. Other computers can detect the chemical ingredients in blood and then instruct medical devices to remove toxic or waste substances, or to add compounds that will help the blood do its work. Computers can also help a person hear by stimulating nerves in response to electronic impulses coming through a small microphone.

In some cases, computers even control man-made organs inside the body, such as an artificial heart; most substitute organs, however, consist of a computerized machine that is too large to fit inside the body but is connected to it with tubes. Researchers hope soon to make life-size computerized organs that will outperform the real ones.

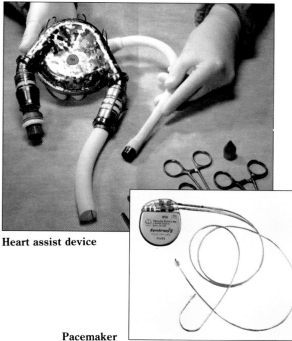

Heart assist device

Pacemaker

Aiding the heart

When the heart does not beat rhythmically, doctors may implant a pacemaker under the skin of the shoulder or abdomen. This computerized machine sends regular electrical impulses to the heart muscle.

If the heart begins to fail, it may be aided by an implanted heart assist device that pumps blood through the heart.

Helping the pancreas

An artificial pancreas system *(below)* reads blood sugar levels, then adds insulin or glucose as the body requires it.

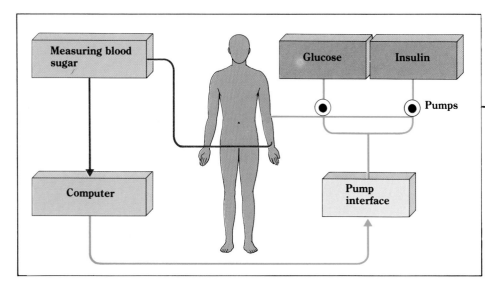

Moving the arm

An artificial arm senses electrical impulses in the shoulder muscle. A battery within the arm then amplifies the impulse to move the elbow and the wrist.

Improving hearing

A computerized hearing aid picks up sounds using an external sensor, converts them to electrical impulses, and stimulates nerves to the brain.

Implanted receiver
Sensor
Electrode

Assisting surgery

During heart or lung operations, blood bypasses the heart and filters through a heart-lung machine *(right)*, which removes carbon dioxide and adds oxygen.

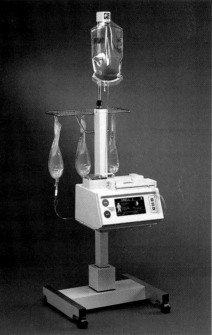

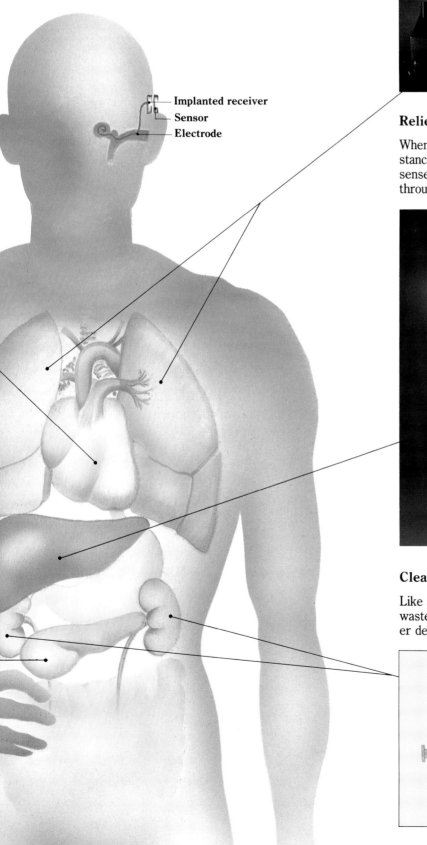

Relieving the liver

When the liver cannot completely filter toxic substances from the blood, a hemoperfusion filter senses the level of toxins, then routes blood through a cleansing device.

Cleaning the blood

Like a real kidney, a hemodialysis machine filters waste products out of the bloodstream. A computer determines the flow of blood.

How Do Satellites Map the Earth?

Computer images of the Earth, as seen from orbit, have changed the way that geologists, ecologists, cartographers, and other researchers view the planet. Most of these images are produced by Landsat satellites, five of which have been launched since 1972.

Each Landsat (two are still operating) circles the Earth about 440 miles up, swinging from North Pole to South Pole and passing over each part of the Earth's surface every 16 days. With each orbit, a satellite concentrates on a single 115-mile-wide north-to-south strip of the Earth below. Instead of using cameras, the Landsats have a system of sensors that in the newer satellites are called thematic mappers (TMs). Within the TMs are scanning mirrors that tilt back and forth, picking up light reflected from the Earth's surface. This light passes through an optical system to a set of detectors that record the wavelengths and intensities of the light waves they receive, including the infrared light that is invisible to human eyes. A computer then converts this information into digital code and transmits it through radio waves to an Earth station. There, the digital signals are changed back into images.

The result is a remarkable graphic representation of portions of the Earth, showing rivers, cities, forests, fields, glaciers, and more. Landsat images are especially helpful to scientists who study forests, the spread of agriculture, and changes in the cleanliness of the environment.

Inside the thematic mapper

The thematic mapper's scanning mirror moves back and forth to pick up light from Earth. The optical system sends the light to detectors in seven wavelength bands.

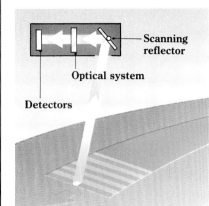

Scanning reflector

Optical system

Detectors

The Earth in color

From 440 miles up, Landsat's thematic mapper can pick out details as small as 30 yards across. The satellite's detectors can register light waves far into the infrared, allowing scientists to glean information unavailable from a regular photograph.

A digital image of southern Florida shows buildings in Miami *(light blue)* and healthy vegetation *(red and purple).*

A relay satellite passes information from Landsat to an Earth station. Unlike Landsat, the relay satellite remains above a single place on Earth.

The flow of image data

Information, or raw data, transmitted from Landsat has to go through a process that renders it into clear pictures. The sequence begins when the receiving antenna on Earth passes the raw data from the relay station to recording devices that use high-density magnetic tape. After computers smooth out irregularities in the transmission, the data is transferred to computer-compatible tape. A laser-beam recorder transfers the data to graphic form, eventually creating a slide.

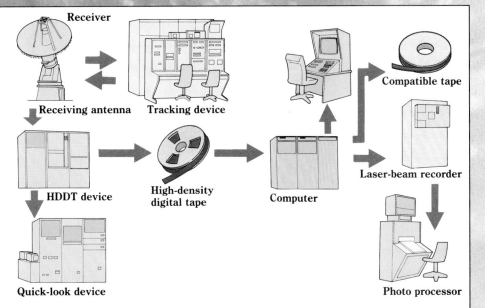

Receiver

Receiving antenna   Tracking device

HDDT device

High-density digital tape

Computer

Quick-look device

Compatible tape

Laser-beam recorder

Photo processor

How Do Space Probes Communicate with Earth?

When *Voyager 1* and *Voyager 2* were launched into deep space in 1977, their designers knew that the space probes would have to maintain flawless communication with Earth or they would be lost. On a mission to and beyond the four large outer planets of the Solar System, both Voyagers were controlled by radio signals from Earth that transmitted instructions to the probes' on-board computers. Those computers, in turn, sent back to Earth data collected during planetary encounters as well as regular signals on the condition of the Voyagers' internal systems.

By the time the probes reached Jupiter, 390 million miles from Earth, signals were taking 35 minutes to travel one way. That made it impossible to have the probe perform a task at the instant a command was given on Earth. Instead, commands were generally prerecorded and sent to the spacecraft in advance. A computer on board stored the commands and relayed them to the appropriate parts at a preset time.

As the Voyagers sped farther from Earth (they are now beyond the orbit of Pluto), their transmissions became increasingly faint. Therefore, an on-board computer grouped the bits of information together so they could be distinguished from the random radio noise that normally can be found in space.

The Deep Space Network

Communications with the Voyager spacecraft are sent and received by three stations on Earth. Known as the Deep Space Network and separated by about 120° of longitude, the stations are in Madrid, Spain; Canberra, Australia; and Goldstone, California. Each has an antenna 70 yards in diameter.

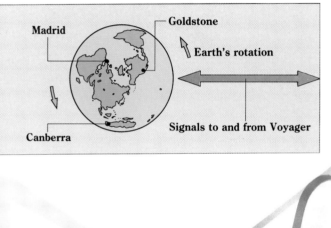

Madrid

Goldstone

Earth's rotation

Signals to and from Voyager

Canberra

● **Message to Voyager**

Scientists measure the time it takes to transmit a signal to the spacecraft and get it back again. They then know how far in advance to relay instructions telling the probe when to make observations and when to change its speed or attitude.

● **Message to Earth**

Signals describing the probe's status and observations took 2¾ hours to reach Earth by the time *Voyager 2* reached Uranus.

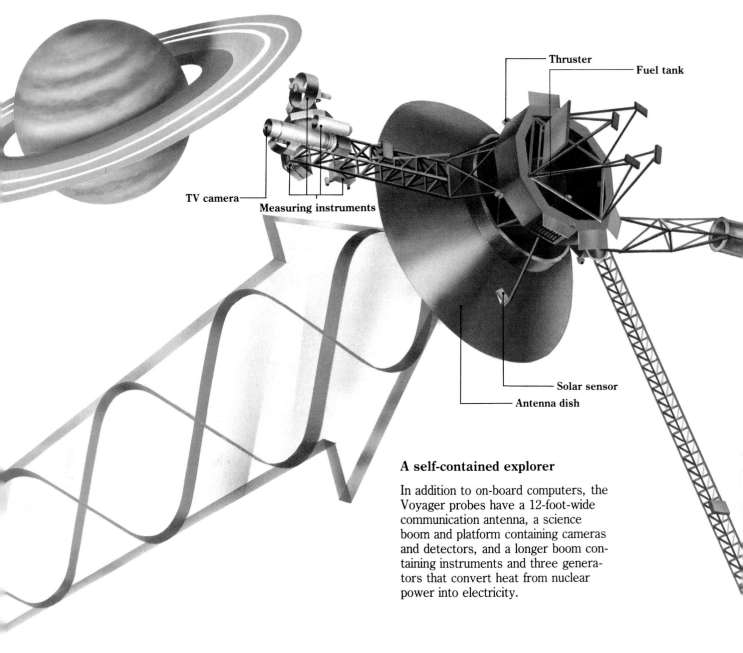

Thruster

Fuel tank

TV camera

Measuring instruments

Solar sensor

Antenna dish

A self-contained explorer

In addition to on-board computers, the Voyager probes have a 12-foot-wide communication antenna, a science boom and platform containing cameras and detectors, and a longer boom containing instruments and three generators that convert heat from nuclear power into electricity.

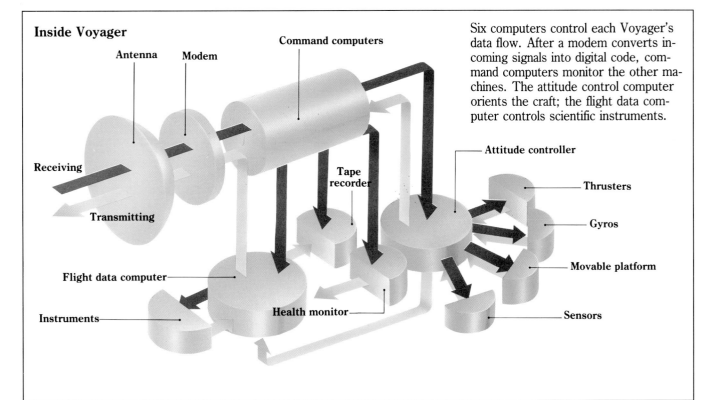

Inside Voyager

Antenna

Modem

Command computers

Six computers control each Voyager's data flow. After a modem converts incoming signals into digital code, command computers monitor the other machines. The attitude control computer orients the craft; the flight data computer controls scientific instruments.

Receiving

Transmitting

Tape recorder

Attitude controller

Thrusters

Gyros

Movable platform

Flight data computer

Instruments

Health monitor

Sensors

How Do Cruise Missiles Fly?

Cruise missiles—jet-propelled, bomb-carrying weapons—are designed to fly very low to avoid being detected by ordinary radar. This means they have to stay within a hundred feet of the ground, skimming over the contours of the land, even soaring up over tall buildings and descending again where the buildings are low.

To do this, engineers program the missile's on-board computer with an ideal flight path, a map of the ground it will cover. For this flight path, the terrain along the route is divided into sections about 100 yards square. Information on the location and height of each square is recorded in the on-board computer. When the missile is launched it measures the distance to the ground with radar and air-pressure sensors. Then it compares this with the flight path. If the computer finds that the missile is not directly on its ideal path, it calls for a course correction. Once the missile is within a few miles of its goal, a photographic guidance system takes over.

Eyes on the ground

When a cruise missile gets close to its target, its camera begins to photograph the ground below. Comparing this information with a map stored in its memory, the missile can determine how far off course it is and send signals for course correction to the automatic pilot.

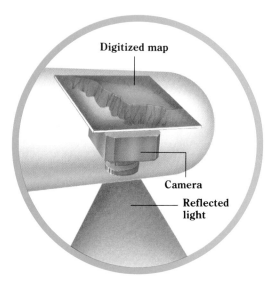

Hugging the land

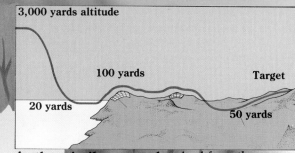

As the missile approaches land from the sea, it lowers its altitude and flies close to the ground to evade detection by radar.

Glossary

Adder circuit: A computer circuit that adds pairs of numbers, can accept a carry-over from a previous column, and carries digits into the next column. Also, **Half adder:** An adder circuit that is incapable of accepting a carry-over as it calculates a sum.

Address: The location of a specific cell in a computer's memory.

Algorithm: A finite set of instructions for solving a particular mathematical problem or performing a specific analytical task.

Amplifier: A device that increases the amplitude of a sound wave.

Amplitude: The height of a sound wave; it determines the strength of the audio signal.

Analog data: Information that is continuous, without well-defined breaks or steps.

Analog/digital (A/D) converter: A device that breaks continuous analog signals into a string of digital signals.

Arithmetic Logic Unit (ALU): The part of the central processing unit that performs calculations.

Artificial Intelligence (AI): The branch of computer science that studies how computers can mimic human thought processes.

Assembly language: A low-level programming language.

Balancing filter: A device that smoothes out the breaks between digital signals produced by a computer.

Band compression: A technique in which a digitized video image is stripped of some detail, creating a signal simple enough to be carried across telephone lines.

Binary code: A number system using base 2 in which numbers are represented by 0s and 1s—rather than standard base 10.

Bit: The smallest unit of information a computer can hold.

Buffer: Memory circuits that temporarily store data.

Byte: A collection of eight bits.

Central Processing Unit (CPU): The part of a computer that interprets and executes programs.

Changed bit coding: A system of storing data on magnetic disks in which the meaning of each magnetic signal depends on the previous signal.

Codec or coder/decoder: An instrument that converts analog video images into signals for transmission over telephone lines.

Code table: A key used to translate letters and punctuation marks into binary symbols.

Command: A statement, such as PRINT or COPY, that sets in motion a preprogrammed sequence of instructions to a computer.

Compiler: A program that translates a programming language into machine language, which the computer can understand.

Computer chip: A small piece of silicon onto which an integrated circuit, consisting of transistors and other electronic components, has been imprinted.

Computer network: A number of computers linked together; such linkage allows each individual computer easy access to information stored in the other computers.

Constant bit coding: A system of storing data on magnetic disks in which each magnetic signal has a meaning independent of the preceding signal.

Constant difference: A method for calculating the value of any mathematical equation in which the answer increases in constant proportion to the variables entered into the equation.

Control unit or controller: The part of the CPU that directs the activity of various parts of a computer in accordance with the directions given in a program.

Count area: The part of a magnetic disk that holds the addresses for all records stored on the disk.

Cursor: A marker, usually a blinking light, that indicates the point of action on a display screen.

Debugging: The process of eliminating all errors, or bugs, from a computer program.

Decimal notation: The standard number system, which uses 10 as its base.

Digital data: Information that can be represented by a series of discrete, well-defined values.

Digital synthesizer: A machine that takes sounds and turns them into digital signals that can be understood by a computer.

Diode: A device that only allows current to flow through a circuit in one direction.

Downlink station: A system that receives communication signals relayed from a communications satellite.

Downloading: The transfer of data between computers.

Echo suppressor: A machine that reduces echoes and other noise interference across telephone lines.

Electronic sketchpad: An instrument that allows the transmission of drawings and graphics between computers; often used in teleconferencing.

Facsimile (fax) machine: A machine capable of transmitting printed material over telephone lines.

Fiberoptic communication: The transmission of information by way of laser light propagated through glass fibers.

File: A collection of related information, stored together in a computer memory or peripheral device.

Floppy disk: A small, flexible, and erasable magnetic disk used to store information and programs.

Fractals: A branch of mathematics that deals with irregular shapes, which often resemble the shapes of objects in nature.

Frequency modulation: A technique used to change the wavelength of a sound wave to alter its pitch.

Hard disk: A rigid magnetic storage disk inside the computer.

High-level language: A sophisticated programming language that approximates human speech far more closely than machine or assembly language.

Indexed sequential organization: The storing of information in which a table lists the key for each unit of memory, making it easy to retrieve data from any part of a computer's memory.

Input: Any data or programming fed into a computer.

Input device: Any piece of hardware, such as a keyboard or a punch card reader, that allows the computer to receive data.

Integrated circuit: An electronic circuit containing a large number of transistors, all constructed on the same silicon chip.

Interference: Signals from various sources that obscure the signal from the desired source; also called noise.

Interpreter: A program that translates and executes a high-level programming language into machine language, performing the translation one line at a time.

Key: An identification symbol assigned by a computer to a specific record within its memory; the key allows the computer to quickly find and identify the record.

Level converter: A device that allows two normally incompatible computers to exchange information.

Light-emitting diode (LED): A semiconductor device that turns on a light when current passes through it.

Liquid crystal display (LCD): A display screen, commonly used in computers, containing a clear liquid that becomes opaque wherever electrical current is applied to it.

Logarithm: An exponent to which a given number, called the base, must be raised to produce a desired number; large numbers can be multiplied or divided by adding or subtracting their logarithms.

Logic chip: An integrated circuit devoted to performing mathematical calculations.

Machine language: The binary instructions—0 or 1, on or off—that are understood by a computer.

Magnetic disk: A disk that stores information as a series of magnetic pulses.

Magnetic head: A device that magnetizes hard and floppy disks for information storage.

Medium memory: Any material, such as floppy disks, on which a computer can store information.

Megabyte: 1,048,576 bytes; equal to 8,388,608 bits.

Memory: The part of a computer devoted to storing data and programs. **Random-access memory, or read-and-write memory (RAM),** refers to memory space in which the user can store and alter information. **Read-only memory (ROM),** also called **primary memory,** refers to memory containing permanent information and programs that cannot be altered.

Memory card: A card containing RAM circuits that can be added to a small computer to increase its power.

Memory chip: An integrated circuit to store data and programs.

Memory unit: The part of the central processing unit devoted to storing programs and data.

Microprocessor: A single computer chip that contains an entire central processing unit.

Modem or **modulator/demodulator:** A device that links computers across ordinary telephone lines, fiberoptic cables, or radio frequencies.

Monitor: A television-like screen on which a computer can display data.

Neurocomputer: A computer that is modeled after the interaction of neurons in the human brain.

Neuron: An individual brain cell; also the name given to the circuits in a neurocomputer.

Operating system: A master program, stored on a computer's hard disk, that controls all programs run on the computer.

Operation: A single task performed by a computer, such as adding or subtracting two numbers.

Output: Information that is sent by the computer to the user or to storage.

Output device: Any hardware, such as a printer or monitor, on which a computer can display the results of its work.

Packet switching: The process by which a digitized message is broken up into small units called packets and transmitted across a computer network.

Parallel (pipeline) processing: The handling of more than one piece of information at a time by a computer; a method much faster than processing one bit of information at a time.

Pattern recognition: The process of comparing the shapes of words and letters to those stored in a computer's memory in an attempt to identify them.

Peripheral: Any piece of hardware, such as a disk drive, or monitor, used for the input or output of information.

Phonemes: The smallest elements of sound into which spoken words can be broken.

Photodetector: A device that triggers an electric signal when it detects light.

Photodiode: A semiconducting device that turns pulses of light into electronic signals.

Pixel: One of the thousands of picture elements into which a computer screen is divided in order to display pictures.

Program: Instructions that tell a computer how to perform a task.

Programming language: A set of symbols, usually combining words, numbers, and abbreviations, that is used in programming.

Radar: A system for studying a distant object by bouncing radio waves off its surface, commonly used for gauging distances.

Raw data: Output from a computer that has to be refined or enhanced before any useful information can be gleaned from it.

Record: Any piece of information located within a file.

Register: A location in a computer's CPU that can temporarily store a number or perform some mathematical operation.

Relay: An electronic switch that may be either open or closed.

Resistor: A device that blocks the flow of current from moving through a circuit.

ROM card: A card containing ROM circuits that allows a small computer to perform specific functions, such as spellchecking.

Scanner: A machine that uses a beam of laser light to read bar codes. Also: A machine that takes graphic material, such as a photograph or a diagram, and converts it into digital signals.

Semiconductor: A material, such as silicon, that can either conduct or block the flow of electricity.

Sensor: A device designed to detect a certain type of radiation, such as radar waves or visible light.

Sequential processing: The handling of only one bit of information at a time by a computer.

Silicon: A semiconducting element from which computer chips are made.

Software: Any instructions, such as a program, that tell a computer what to do.

Sorting: The process of organizing data in a specific manner, be it alphabetically, numerically, or in some other sequence.

Sound spectrograph: A machine that performs acoustic analysis of sound.

Spectrum analyzer: A device that takes sound and breaks it up into its component waves.

Stereo digital photogrammetric station (SDPS): A machine that uses photographs of an object taken at different angles to produce a three-dimensional picture of the object.

Transistor: An electronic circuit that is made of semiconducting material.

Transponder: An instrument in a communications satellite that both amplifies the signals it receives and sends them to their destinations back on earth.

Uplink station: A system for sending communication signals from earth to a communications satellite.

Utility program: A program that performs simple tasks such as adding numbers or sorting through a list of data.

Vector processing: A way of parallel-processing information in which data is arranged into two-dimensional arrays, or vectors.

Very-large-scale integration: The placement of from 100,000 to 1 million transistors on a single computer chip.

Virus: A program that distorts or takes over a preexisting computer program and then copies itself onto some additional programs called up by the computer.

Voice recognition system: A computer that "understands" spoken words by breaking down and analyzing their basic sounds.

Voice synthesizer: A machine that imitates the human voice.

Wave-form: A combination of individual sound waves that duplicates a given sound.

Wavelength: The width of a given sound wave; it determines the sound's pitch.

Index

LCC (leadless chip carrier), *23*
Legs, robotic, *99*
Leibniz, Baron Gottfried Wilhelm von, 8; calculator invented by, *9*
Letters, electronic mail (E-mail), *116-117*
Level converters, use of, *91*
Light, laser: bar codes scanned by, *86-87;* fiberoptic cables guiding, *124-125*
Light-emitting diodes (LEDs): in mouse, *34, 35;* in pen-type scanners, *87*
Liver, computerized assistance for, *139*
Local area networks (LANs), 108
Logarithms, inventor of, 8
Logic chips, 22, *23*
Logic elements (gates), *21, 28;* in adder circuits, 28, *29*
Loom, Jacquard, 10, *11*

M

Machine language, 50; translation into, *51*
Magnetic data storage, *19, 36-37, 56-57*
Mail, electronic (E-mail), *116-117*
Mainframe computer, architecture of, *18-19*
MALTRON layout of keys, *33*
Management functions of computers, 93
Manipulator (robotic hand), *98*
Maps and mapping, computer, *76-77;* Landsat satellites for, *140-141;* weather, *135*
Mark I calculator, *14*
Marketing functions of computers, 93
Mauchly, John, 14
Mechanical vs. optical mouse, *34-35*
Medical uses of computers, *138-139*
Memory, 18, *30-31;* CD-ROM, *95*
Memory cards for pocket computers, *91*
Memory chips, 22
Message-display vs. tone-only pagers, 122, *123*
Message handling system (MHS), 116, 117
Meteorology, computer use in, *134-135*
Microprocessors: chips, *16-17, 22, 23;* and keyboard, *32, 33;* multiple, *42-43;* robotic eye with, *99*
Missiles, cruise, *144*
Mobile phone calls, *120-121*
Mobile robots, problem of, *99*
Models and simulations, computer. *See* Simulations and models, computer
Modems (modulator/demodulators), use of, 118, *119;* by pocket computer, *91*
Modulation: in faxing, *115;* frequency modulation, *66*

Motherboard, *22-23*
Motion analysis programs for athletes, *136-137*
Mouse, *34-35*
Movies, special effects for, *80-81*
Music making, *66-67*

N

Napier, John, 8
Napier's rods, *5, 8*
Navigation system, on-board, in automobile, *103*
Negative-channel metal-oxide semiconductor (n-MOS), *22*
Nerve cells (neurons) of human brain, *45*
Networks, computer, *108-129;* business computers, *92-93;* car phones, *120-121;* data transfer between computers, *91, 118-119;* electronic mail, *116-117;* fax machines, *114-115;* fiberoptic communications, *124-125;* pagers, electronic, *122-123;* picture phones, *126-127;* satellites, communications, *128-129;* teleconferencing, *112-113;* telephone lines, voice transmission through, *110-111*
Neurocomputers, *44-45*
Neurons (nerve cells) of human brain, *45*
n-MOS (negative-channel metal-oxide semiconductor), *22*

O

Offices, computer use in, *92-93*
Optical fibers, communication by, *124-125*
Optical mouse, *34*
Organs, artificial, *138-139*
OR gate, *28*
Output devices, 18, *19;* for pocket computers, *90-91;* printers, working of, *38-39*

P

Pacemaker, *138*
Packet switching, *118-119*
Pagers, electronic, *122-123*
Painting of automobiles, robot use in, *101*
Pancreas system, artificial, *138*
Parallel (pipeline) processing, *42-43*
Pascal, Blaise, 8, *9;* quoted, 9
Pascaline (adding machine), *4-5, 8-9*
Passwords, 106; possible, number of, *chart* 107
PCBs (printed circuit boards), *20-21;* motherboard, *22-23*
PCs. *See* Personal computers

Peripherals, 19
Personal computers, *19;* E-mail, use of, 116, *117;* graphics, 70; motherboard, *22-23;* pocket computer's communication with, *91;* as word processors, *58-59*
Personal identification numbers (PINs), 88, 89
Personnel functions of computers, 93
Phones. *See* Telephones and telephone lines
Photodetectors: bar codes scanned by, *86;* in mouse, *34*
Photodiodes: in fiberoptic communication, *125;* in mouse, *35;* in scanners, *87*
Picture elements. *See* Pixels
Picture phones, *126-127*
Pictures: electronic publishing of, *94-95;* faxing, *114-115. See also* Graphics, computer
Pilot training, flight simulator for, *82-83*
PINs (personal identification numbers), 88, 89
Pipeline (parallel) processing, *42-43*
Pixels, 70; in electronic publishing, *95;* in faxed images, 114, *115;* in TV vs. videophone images, *127*
Pocket calendars, *91*
Pocket computers, *90-91*
Pollution from automobiles, computerized control of, 102
Primary memory, *30-31*
Printed circuit boards (PCBs), *20-21;* motherboard, *22-23*
Printers, *19, 38-39;* pocket computers and, *90-91*
Production area of business, computer use in, 93
Production lines, robot use on, *100-101*
Program counter, 24
Programming languages, *50-51;* programs in, 51
Programs and software. *See* Software and programs
Prosthetic (artificial) limbs, *138*
Publishing, electronic, *94-95*
Punch cards, *4-5, 10, 11;* census tabulating machines's system, *12-13*

Q

QFP (IC package), *23*
QWERTY layout of keys, *33*

R

Radio signals, communications with: cellular phones, *120-121;* pagers,

Staff for
UNDERSTANDING SCIENCE & NATURE

Editorial Directors: Patricia Daniels, Karin Kinney
Text Editor: Allan Fallow
Writer: Mark Galan
Assistant Editor/Research: Elizabeth Thompson
Editorial Assistant: Louisa Potter
Production Manager: Prudence G. Harris
Senior Copy Coordinator: Jill Lai Miller
Production: Celia Beattie
Library: Louise D. Forstall
Computer Composition: Deborah G. Tait (Manager), Monika D.
　　Thayer, Janet Barnes Syring, Lillian Daniels

Special Contributors, Text: Margery duMond, Patricia N. Holland,
　　Gina Maranto, Brooke C. Stoddard, Mark Washburn
Research: Patricia N. Holland
Design/Illustration: Antonio Alcalá, Caroline Brock,
　　Nicholas Fasciano, Yvonne Gensurowsky-SRW, Inc., Catherine
　　D. Mason, Stephen Wagner
Photography: Evan Sheppard, Elizabeth Kupersmith
Index: Barbara L. Klein
Acknowledgments: EOSAT; Fresenius USA, Inc.; Museum of Amer-
　　ican History, Smithsonian Institution; Pacesetters Systems, Inc.;
　　Shiley Incorporated; Spoken Language Systems Group, MIT Lab-
　　oratory for Computer Science; Thermo Cardiosystems, Inc.;
　　Robert Wilhelmson, National Center for Supercomputing Applica-
　　tions, University of Illinois, Urbana

Consultants:

Jon Eklund is curator of electronic computers at the National
Museum of American History, Smithsonian Institution,
Washington, D.C.
Rachelle S. Heller is professor of computer science in the Depart-
ment of Electrical Engineering & Computer Science, George
Washington University, Washington, D.C.

Library of Congress Cataloging-in-Publication Data

Computer age.
　　　p.　cm. — (Understanding science & nature)
　　Includes index.
　　Summary: Describes, in a question and answer format, the
workings of computers, from early calculating machines to supercomputers, from personal computers to neural networks.
　　ISBN 0-8094-9670-4 (trade). — ISBN 0-8094-9671-2 (lib. bdg.)
　　1. Computers—Juvenile literature. [1. Computers—Miscella-
nea.　2. Questions and answers.]
I. Time-Life Books.　II. Series.
QA76.23.C66　1992
004—dc20
　　　　　　　　　　　　　　　　　91-41745
　　　　　　　　　　　　　　　　　CIP
　　　　　　　　　　　　　　　　　AC

TIME-LIFE for CHILDREN ™

Publisher: Robert H. Smith
Associate Publisher and Managing Editor: Neil Kagan
Editorial Directors: Jean Burke Crawford, Patricia Daniels,
　　Allan Fallow, Karin Kinney, Sara Mark
Editorial Coordinator: Elizabeth Ward
Director of Marketing: Margaret Mooney
Product Manager: Cassandra Ford
Assistant Product Manager: Shelley L. Shimkus
Business Manager: Lisa Peterson
Assistant Business Manager: Patricia Vanderslice
Administrative Assistant: Rebecca C. Christoffersen
Special Contributor: Jacqueline A. Ball

Original English translation by International Editorial Services Inc./
C. E. Berry

Second printing. Printed in U.S.A.
Published simultaneously in Canada.
Time Life Inc. is a wholly owned subsidiary of
THE TIME INC. BOOK COMPANY.
TIME-LIFE is a trademark of Time Warner Inc. U.S.A.
For subscription information, call 1-800-621-7026.